ART
is
Leadership

"To lead is to make art to risk, to connect, to create possibility where none existed before."

ART
is
Leadership

Formation, Not Performance

DAVID S. MORGAN

Horizon Echo Publishing.

CONTENTS

ONE
The Incomplete Field

Leadership's century of scholarship, and why the artistic half remained outside the frame

You already know something is missing.

Not intelligence. Not competence. Not experience or strategy or will. You have spent years, decades, becoming skilled, responsible, and effective. You can plan, analyze, execute, communicate.

You have read the books.

Attended the programs.

Internalized the frameworks.

And yet.

There are moments when none of it holds. The room goes tense after bad news, and everyone looks down instead of up. A conversation tilts off course, and you cannot recover it. A decision is technically correct, but somehow leaves people smaller. You stand in front of your team with the right words and the right data and the right intention, and the room does not move.

You notice it in your body first. A tightness in the chest. A flicker of something, not panic exactly, but the recognition that what you have is not what this moment needs. Your mind races through options, but the options all feel cognitive, and the problem is not cognitive. The problem is in the space between you and the people in front of you. Something is supposed to be flowing there: trust, meaning, presence, and it is not.

Not because you failed.

Because something the moment required was not available to you.

You could feel what was needed.

You could not produce it.

This is not a failure of preparation.

It is a gap in what you were prepared for.

And you are not alone in sensing it.

•   •   •

What a Century of Leadership Science Built

For more than a hundred years, leadership scholars have attempted to explain why people follow, why some organizations thrive, and what distinguishes leaders who transform from those who merely manage. The progress has been genuine and substantial.

Trait theory gave way to behavioral models. Behavioral models gave way to situational and contingency frameworks. Transformation replaced transaction. Emotional intelligence entered the conversation.

Complexity science revealed that leadership is distributed, adaptive, relational, emergent.

We now understand that psychological safety matters more than charisma, that networks shape influence more than hierarchy, and that meaning mobilizes people more powerfully than incentives.

This is not a minor achievement. Leadership became a science: complete with competencies, assessments, developmental roadmaps, and empirical rigor. The field gave us tools that elevated leadership practice far beyond the "Great Man" myths of the early twentieth century.

More importantly, it democratized leadership. It showed us that leadership is not a birthright but a practice. Not a personality but a set of learnable behaviors. Not the province of the few but a capacity distributed across systems. This was liberating. It opened the door for millions of people who would never have been considered "leaders" under the old paradigm.

And yet leaders still struggle with familiar challenges. Teams stall even when alignment is high. Competence does not guarantee commitment. Clarity does not create momentum. Some leaders inspire devotion while others, equally capable, evoke only compliance.

The field has reached the edge of what its instruments were designed to capture.

•   •   •

What Got Measured, and What Didn't

Leadership scholarship advanced according to what research methodologies could detect.

Psychology measured traits, cognition, and emotion, so we learned about personality, decision-making, and emotional regulation.

Management science measured strategy, planning, and execution, so we learned about goal-setting, resource allocation, and performance.

Organizational behavior measured coordination, motivation, and culture, so we learned about team dynamics, engagement, and climate.

Each discipline contributed vital insight. None of them were designed to capture the lived, embodied, aesthetic, and symbolic dimensions of leadership: the dimensions that exist in the moment of encounter, where leadership either resonates or falls flat.

You have probably experienced the difference. There are meetings where every agenda item is covered, and nothing actually happened. There are conversations where the right words were spoken, and the other person left feeling less seen, not more. There are presentations where the data was flawless, and the room was unmoved. You could sense what was missing. You just could not find it on any assessment.

Consider what gets measured in typical leadership research: vision clarity scored on Likert scales, communication frequency tracked in surveys, decision quality evaluated by outcomes, emotional intelligence assessed through questionnaires, trust levels reported by followers.

Now consider what these instruments cannot measure.

The quality of a leader's presence when entering a room after layoffs have been announced. The precise timing of when to speak and when to hold silence in a tense negotiation. The somatic awareness that tells a leader their team is performing confidence but feeling doubt. The aesthetic judgment that knows which metaphor will land and which will alienate. The rhythm and pacing that make collaboration feel generative rather than exhausting.

These are not peripheral capacities. They are the ones that determine whether people trust you when it matters.

Leadership scholarship did not ignore them because they are unimportant. It could not detect them yet.

•   •   •

The Asymmetry

To test whether this gap was merely anecdotal, whether the sense that something was missing reflected reality or simply personal bias, I examined seventeen influential sources spanning three decades of leadership scholarship. The sources represented the field's strongest voices: complexity and adaptive leadership, innovation and embodiment, critical perspectives that challenge heroic models, and ethical leadership emphasizing stakeholder responsibility.

Across more than one hundred and twenty coded excerpts, a pattern emerged.

The results confirmed what leaders already feel.

Three clusters dominated the dataset. Adaptive and complexity leadership accounted for twenty-one percent of all excerpts, leaders described as enablers of emergence, catalysts of resilience, navigators of turbulence. Enabling practices and structural network dynamics together accounted for another twenty percent. The field has developed sophisticated frameworks for systems thinking, adaptive capacity, and distributed influence.

But three other clusters were strikingly underrepresented. Relational and embodied leadership, leaders as presences whose gestures, tone, posture, and somatic awareness shape encounters, accounted for five percent. Symbolic and meaning-making leadership, leaders as narrators and world-builders who create shared meaning through metaphor, story, and ritual, accounted for two percent. Ethical leadership emphasizing moral imagination accounted for another two percent.

Five percent for the body.

Two percent for meaning.

Two percent for ethics.

Fifty-three excerpts on systems, structures, and complexity.

Eleven on embodiment, symbolism, and ethics.

This is not a balanced field. It is a field that has developed deeply in the domains its methods could capture, and remained thin in precisely the dimensions where leaders struggle most.

•   •   •

The Crisis Is Not in Action. It Is in Being.

People do not follow leaders because of competencies alone.

They follow because of how a leader makes them feel, see, and understand themselves and their world.

They follow because a leader helps them make sense of complexity, find meaning in difficulty, and discover courage they did not know they had.

Think of the last time you walked into a room where you had just heard bad news. No one needed to tell you what had happened. You could feel it before anyone spoke: in the way people avoided eye contact, in the tightness of the air, in your own chest. Leadership in that moment had nothing to do with a model. It had everything to do with how you chose to stand there.

Or think of the opposite: a time when someone walked into a room, and the room changed. Not because of what they said. Because of what they carried. A steadiness. A groundedness. A willingness to be present to difficulty without flinching. You may not have had words for what they did. But your body recognized it instantly.

These are the moments leadership actually happens. Not in the competency framework. Not in the strategic plan. Not in the 360-degree feedback report. But in the live encounter, where everything either lands or falls apart.

And what is needed in those moments is not more information. It is capacity.

The capacity to be fully present without self-protection.

To stand in the weight of bad news without armoring against it, without retreating into a script, without performing composure while the body screams to flee.

The capacity to attune to what is alive in the room and respond to it skillfully.

To feel the doubt beneath the agreement, the grief beneath the compliance, the question no one will ask out loud.

The capacity to offer meaning that resonates, not just clarity that informs.

To say something that lands not just in the mind but in the chest, that gives people language for what they have been feeling but could not name.

The capacity to sense timing, read rhythm, and shape the aesthetic quality of the encounter.

To know that this is not the moment for the announcement, even though the slides are ready, because the room has not yet metabolized what came before.

These capacities cannot be studied into existence. They cannot be acquired through reading, memorized from a framework, or installed through a workshop. They must be formed. Slowly, through sustained practice that changes not what you know but who you are under pressure.

The field built the outer architecture of leadership: the systems, structures, strategies, and skills.

It never had access to the inner architecture: the embodied capacity, aesthetic sensibility, and moral grounding that allow a leader to be fully present when everything is at stake.

Neuroscience research confirms what artists and contemplatives have long known: under pressure, the brain does not default to what it knows. It defaults to what it has practiced. The capacities that remain when cognition fragments are the capacities that were trained below conscious thought: in the nervous system, in the body, in the embodied habits that years of deliberate practice built.

Leadership development trains the prefrontal cortex.

Under threshold conditions, it is the first thing to go offline.

What remains is what was trained beneath it.

And for most leaders, nothing was trained beneath it.

•   •   •

Why the Gap Became a Crisis

For most of the twentieth century, this gap was invisible. It did not need to be visible. Organizations operated with predictable hierarchies. Markets moved slowly enough that strategy could extend years into the future. The environment rewarded efficiency, control, and standardization. In that world, leadership could be studied as a set of behaviors applied to known situations.

That world is gone.

You can feel the difference in your own work. Systems that looked stable yesterday fracture without warning: a supply chain, a team, a funding model, a culture that seemed solid until it wasn't. A low-grade anxiety hums beneath everything, making it harder to think clearly, harder to take risks, harder to distinguish signal from noise. Small decisions cascade in ways no one predicted. Information multiplies, but meaning does not. You are drowning in dashboards and starving for clarity. Transparency makes every misstep visible. Work has shifted from transaction to identity. People no longer commit simply because they are paid. They need to believe the work matters.

Scholars have given this a name. You did not need it. You have been living inside it.

Under these conditions, competence without presence produces distance. Strategy without meaning produces compliance, not commitment. Communication without attunement lands as noise. Vision without aesthetic resonance feels hollow.

The capacities that were once academically illegible are now existentially essential.

Leaders today do not struggle because they do not know what to do. They struggle because they do not know how to hold themselves and others through pressure. They were trained in strategy, communication, decision-making, and performance management. They were not trained in embodied presence, emotional attunement, symbolic meaning-making, or the capacity to hold complexity without collapsing.

•   •   •

Where the Missing Lineage Has Been All Along

Other domains have developed that inner architecture not through theory, but through lived practice. Not through frameworks, but through thresholds that must be crossed. Not through abstraction, but through embodiment that must be cultivated.

Artists have spent centuries refining precisely the capacities leadership scholarship identified but could not train.

This is not an argument that artists are leaders, nor that leaders should become artists. Many brilliant artists have no interest in leading organizations. Artistic mastery does not predict leadership effectiveness. Leaders will not suddenly start painting, dancing, or composing.

This is an argument about transferable capacities.

Consider what happens when a promising manager is promoted into a senior leadership role. They are given training in strategic thinking, performance management, communication skills, and emotional intelligence. They learn frameworks for decision-making, models for motivation, and tools for delegation. All of this is valuable. But none of it prepares them for the experience of being watched, of having every gesture and tone interpreted as a signal. None of it trains them to hold the weight of responsibility when the room is looking to them for steadiness they do not feel. None of it builds the capacity to remain present when their own identity as a leader is under threat. Where is the developmental lineage for that? It is not in leadership scholarship. It is in the studio, the rehearsal room, and the stage.

Artists have developed, through rigorous, disciplined practice, specific ways of being that leadership now desperately needs but has no systematic way to cultivate.

What artists have built, leadership now requires.

Presence under pressure.

Artists train to remain fully present when fully exposed: performing before audiences who will see every hesitation, creating under scrutiny, collaborating when stakes are high. A dancer learns to recover from a stumble without collapsing the performance. A musician plays through memory lapses. An actor stays in character when a scene partner forgets their lines. This is not talent. It is trained capacity to regulate the nervous system when visibility is high and consequences are real.

Attunement to others and context.

A conductor hears when a single voice in a choir of sixty goes flat. A dancer feels when their partner is off-balance before the stumble occurs. An improviser senses when the scene needs escalation and when it needs silence. This is not empathy as sentiment. It is an embodied skill in reading the relational field and adjusting in real time.

Aesthetic judgment.

A filmmaker knows which scene to cut and which to extend. A poet knows which word carries the right resonance. A designer knows when simplicity will clarify and when it will flatten. This is trained sensitivity to form, rhythm, and impact: knowing intuitively what will move people and what will alienate them.

Symbolic fluency.

A muralist transforms a blank wall into a site of collective identity. A playwright gives audiences language for experiences they could not articulate. A photographer frames reality in ways that reveal what was always there but never noticed. This is not decoration. It is the disciplined practice of creating meaning through symbol and story.

Rhythm and timing.

Jazz musicians improvise together because they have trained to listen and respond faster than thought. Choreographers know when dancers need rest and when they need to be pushed. This is cultivated sensitivity to temporal flow: knowing when to lead and when to follow, when to push for closure and when to hold space for emergence.

Improvisation within structure.

Actors build scenes in real time, trusting that coherence will emerge from interaction. Jazz soloists take risks knowing they might fail, but are trained to recover. Designers embrace constraints and turn them into breakthroughs. This is disciplined responsiveness: the capacity to sense, adjust, and create when prediction is impossible.

Resilience under exposure.

Writers whose manuscripts were rejected dozens of times kept writing. Performers who were booed returned to the stage. Painters whose work was ignored for decades continued creating. This is trained capacity to sustain commitment when exposure is inevitable, and criticism is real.

These are not vague artistic qualities. They are specific, learnable, trainable capacities that artists develop through deliberate practice, and that can be adapted for leaders without requiring them to become artists.

•　　•　　•

Artistry, Not Creativity

It is essential to distinguish this from the integration of creativity into leadership, which has already happened through design thinking, innovation labs, brainstorming techniques, and creative problem-solving frameworks. Those contributions are valuable. They focus on generating ideas.

This book is about artistry, not creativity.

You may have experienced the difference without having language for it. The innovation workshop that produced forty ideas on sticky notes and changed nothing about how anyone led the next morning. The brainstorm that left the room energized and the culture untouched. The design sprint that solved a problem and developed no one. Creativity generates possibilities. It does not form the person who must carry them into rooms where everything is at stake.

Creativity asks: How do we generate new possibilities?

Artistry asks: How do we become the kind of people who can hold those possibilities and bring them into being?

Creativity is cognitive. Artistry is ontological. Creativity produces outcomes. Artistry forms capacities. Creativity happens in workshops. Artistry is cultivated through sustained practice that changes who you are.

These capacities do not come from frameworks. They come from practice: sustained, disciplined practice under constraint. And that practice has been refined over centuries in artistic disciplines.

* * *

The Two Meanings of Performance

The word "performance" has two meanings.

One is execution. Hitting targets. Delivering results. Managing output. This is the performance leadership has measured for a century.

The other is expression. The live act of making meaning visible to others. This is the performance of the actor on stage, the musician in concert, the dancer in motion, the speaker who shifts a room not through content but through presence.

Leaders are already performing in this second sense. Every time they stand before a team, they are offering presence that others will interpret, respond to, and be shaped by. They rehearse before town halls. They read rooms. They modulate their energy. They try to project confidence without arrogance, openness without weakness, steadiness without rigidity. They work to create a felt sense of possibility, not just through words, but through how they stand, how they listen, how they hold silence.

And it is performance without training.

Execution is one kind of performance. Expression is the other. One builds results. The other builds devotion. One moves work. The other moves people. One can be managed through systems. The other can only be cultivated through practice.

For centuries, one discipline has specialized in training people to perform meaning under pressure. To hold the emotional field of a room. To embody presence that allows others to feel, see, and imagine differently. To work with symbol, rhythm, timing, and emotional precision. To sustain vulnerability without collapsing. To make meaning visible through form.

That discipline is not management. It is artistry.

•　　•　　•

Completion, Not Critique

This book does not argue that leadership scholarship failed. It argues that leadership scholarship succeeded brilliantly within the boundaries of what its paradigm allowed, and now stands at the threshold of its next evolution.

The century of leadership research gave us essential foundations. We know that leadership is not about traits but about behaviors that can be learned. We know it is not heroic but distributed. We know it is not about control but about enabling emergence. These insights transformed how we lead.

But they reached the edge of what their methods could capture. And at that edge, we find the capacities that live in embodiment, aesthetics, symbol, and presence.

Leadership is not broken.

It is half built.

The first century of leadership taught us how to perform. The next will teach us how to resonate. The first gave us the outer architecture: systems, structures, strategies, skills. The next will integrate the inner architecture: presence, attunement, rhythm, aesthetics, and ethics.

When you pair the sophistication of complexity leadership with the embodied presence of a dancer, when you combine the network orchestration of distributed leadership with the attunement of a conductor, when you integrate the enabling practices of adaptive leadership with the aesthetic judgment of a filmmaker, when you bring together the resilience demanded by turbulence with the improvisation practiced by jazz musicians, you get leadership that is finally whole.

Not leadership that performs wholeness. Leadership that has been formed into it.

•   •   •

The Turn

The question, then, is not whether these capacities matter. You already know they do. You have felt their presence in the leaders who changed you, and their absence in the moments when leadership failed despite everything being "right."

The question is where they come from. How they are built. And why the field that has spent a century studying leadership never found the developmental pathway that has been training them all along.

Here is what I have come to believe, after thirty years of watching artists and leading organizations:

Under extreme pressure, the brain does not rise to the occasion.

It falls to its highest level of practiced capacity.

What you trained deeply enough to become automatic, in your breath, your posture, your attention, your embodied habits, is what remains when thinking fails.

Artists know this. They have always known it. Every dancer who trained for years to hold presence under the audience's gaze, every musician who practiced until the instrument became an extension of the nervous system, every improviser who learned to act before the mind could plan, they were forming the capacities that remain when cognition is not enough.

Leadership development has never systematically built these capacities. It has built knowledge, skill, strategy, and frameworks. It has trained the thinking mind. It has not trained what remains when thinking fails.

That is the gap this book addresses. Not by offering another framework. Not by providing a competency model dressed in artistic language. But by entering the world of artists from inside, through research into lived experience across sixteen disciplines, and showing what artistry actually builds in the human being who practices it.

If any of this feels familiar, it is because you have already been here. You have stood in rooms where capacity mattered more than competence. You have felt moments where presence determined everything and strategy determined nothing. You have sensed, in your body, that leadership requires something you were never given a way to build.

What follows is an encounter with the places where it has been formed: quietly, rigorously, for centuries.

TWO

The Universals of Artistry

**The invisible journey beneath technique,
talent, and performance**

What we noticed first wasn't skill.

People admire finished art: the painting under lights, the choreography on opening night, the scene that makes strangers cry, the song that becomes a memory for millions. But the finished product tells almost nothing of the interior transformation that produced it.

What is visible is the outcome. What is invisible is what it took to become the kind of person who could make it.

Walk into any gallery opening. Stand in front of a canvas: bold strokes, colors that vibrate against each other, a composition that holds your attention without demanding it. Collectors murmur about technique. Critics mention influences. The artist stands in the corner, wine glass in hand, nodding politely.

But no one sees what the artist sees when they look at that canvas.

They don't see the forty-seven failed attempts before this one. The months when every brushstroke felt like lying. The morning they almost quit because their hands couldn't execute what their mind could see. The night they broke through, not because they got better, but because they finally stopped trying to control what the painting wanted to become. The canvas doesn't show that journey. It only shows the arrival.

This is true across every art form. The dancer on stage, elegant, precise, seemingly weightless, does not reveal the years spent learning to stay in their body when every instinct screamed to leave it. The jazz musician mid-solo, fluid, responsive, building something that sounds inevitable, does not broadcast the terror of improvisation or the thousands of hours learning to listen faster than they think. The novelist whose book sits on your nightstand doesn't include footnotes about the chapters written in despair, the characters who refused to cooperate, the identity crisis that happened when the story revealed truths they weren't ready to claim.

Art hides its own making.

And this creates a dangerous illusion: that artists are born, not built. That creativity is a gift, not a transformation. That some people have it and others don't.

The research tells a different story.

•　　•　　•

What We Were Actually Studying

We examined research into lived experience across sixteen artistic disciplines: dance, music, theater, visual arts, poetry, fiction, film, sculpture, photography, jazz, street art, installation, ceramics, choreography, conducting, and improvisation.

We weren't studying their work.

We were studying their becoming.

We drew from memoirs, interviews, ethnographies, performance studies, embodied cognition research, and first-person accounts of artistic development, research that examines the lived experience of artists from the inside.

And we asked one question, over and over:

What did artistry do to you?

Not "What did you learn?" Not "What techniques did you master?" But: How did the practice of making art change the way you perceive, feel, decide, relate, and exist in the world?

The answers, across disciplines, across cultures, across levels of mastery, described the same interior journey. Not metaphorically. Structurally. Not always in the same order. Not always using the same language. But always with the same psychological shape.

•　　•　　•

The Body First

Every artistic journey begins in the body, long before the mind catches up.

Before a dancer understands choreography, they understand the pull of balance. Before a painter understands composition, they understand the resistance of the wrist. Before a singer understands interpretation, they understand vibration in the ribs.

At first, this is confusing. The beginner tries to think their way to good work. A young dancer stands at the barre, watching the instructor demonstrate a simple tendu. It looks easy: slide the foot along the floor, point the toe, return. The dancer's mind catalogues the instructions: engage the core, lengthen the spine, turn out from the hip, keep the shoulders down. They execute the movement. Technically correct. Completely dead.

The instructor stops them. "You're thinking too much. Feel it."

This makes no sense to the beginner. The body doesn't "want" anything. The body follows instructions. The mind decides, the body obeys. That's how it works.

Except in art, that's not how it works.

Then something shifts. It might happen in a single moment or slowly over months. But eventually, the artist stops fighting their body and starts listening to it. A dancer stops trying to push through the movement and starts feeling where it wants to unfold. A singer stops wrestling the breath and discovers that breath knows things the mind doesn't. A sculptor stops forcing the clay and starts responding to what the clay is doing: the way it collapses here, resists there, opens unexpectedly in a third place. A writer stops forcing lines and starts feeling where the sentence wants to land: the rhythm of the thought, the weight of the word, the pause that makes meaning cohere.

The body becomes not an obstacle but a data-rich sensory instrument.

Artists learn to treat sensation as information. They begin to locate truth somatically: this movement collapses my center, something is structurally off. This phrasing releases my throat; something is unlocking. This image tightens my gut. I'm hiding from what wants to be said. This line eases my breath. I've found it.

A dancer who trained at Juilliard for eight years said, "I didn't trust a scene until my stomach dropped. My brain could lie. My gut couldn't."

You cannot make anything real while disconnected from your body. When a performance feels true, it is not because the actor is telling the truth about their life. It is because their nervous system is coherent. There is no gap between what they are feeling and what they are expressing. The body and the work are in alignment.

And here is what makes this capacity rare: most people leave their bodies under pressure. You know this feeling. The meeting turns, the stakes spike, and suddenly your awareness shoots up into your head like an elevator trying to escape. Your shoulders lock. Your breath goes shallow. You become a brain on stilts.

Artists train themselves to do the opposite.

To drop down, not rise up, when pressure arrives.

To stay embodied when the choreography isn't working, when the audience is watching, when the work is failing, when exposure feels unbearable.

From that staying, everything else becomes possible.

•   •   •

The Space Between

After the body comes the world. Not the world in the abstract, but the world in relation.

If the body roots the artist in the self, what comes next roots the artist in the space between selves.

A cellist sits in a string quartet, playing a Brahms piece they've rehearsed for months. They know their part perfectly: every note, every dynamic, every phrase. But something is wrong. The music is technically correct and emotionally flat.

The cellist isn't listening. They're performing their part, executing it, but not hearing the violinist's slight hesitation before the modulation, not sensing the violist's breath pattern, not feeling the moment when all four players need to lean into the dissonance before resolving.

The conductor stops them. "You're playing at each other, not with each other."

The cellist tries again. This time, they don't just play. They listen. They feel the room's energy. They sense the micro-adjustments everyone is making in real time. They let their phrasing bend slightly to accommodate the violinist's interpretation. They breathe with the group.

The music comes alive. Not because anyone played better. Because everyone is attuned.

A jazz improviser cannot choose their next phrase without sensing what the room is holding: the tension the drummer just created, the space the bassist just opened, the energy the audience is carrying. A poet cannot choose a metaphor without sensing the weight silence is already carrying. A filmmaker cannot cut a scene without feeling the emotional temperature of what just happened, not analyzing it intellectually, but sensing it in the body while watching the footage.

Artists learn to detect a held breath before a shift, the sag of a shoulder that changes the tempo of a scene, the hesitation in a collaborator's voice that hints at a different emotional truth, the collective exhale in a room that signals release. These are not skills taught through instruction. They are capacities developed through thousands of hours of practice in relational fields: standing securely in oneself while sensing what the space between holds.

And from this develops a paradox most people never resolve: coordination without conformity, moving together without becoming the same. Sensitivity without fragility, feeling everything without collapsing. Adjustment without self-abandonment, adapting in real time without losing your center.

• • •

Moving With Time

Once the artist can sense the self and sense others, time becomes the next teacher.

Beginners push, always a little ahead or a little behind the moment. The novice dancer anticipates the beat, rushing into the next movement before the current one resolves. The early-stage writer forces the ending because they're tired, not because the story is finished. The inexperienced actor fills every silence because they fear dead air.

Beginners treat time as an enemy: something to race against, something to fill, something to master through control.

Experienced artists learn something different: the moment tells you when to move.

A dancer doesn't take the step when the music says "now," they take it when the accumulated bodily tension demands release. A guitarist doesn't enter because the bar count hits four, they enter because the collective energy crests, and the silence has become unbearable in exactly the right way. A choreographer doesn't finish a phrase because the clock says the rehearsal is over, they finish because the piece has exhaled and the next breath hasn't arrived yet.

Time becomes felt, not measured.

A choreographer described it this way: "My job isn't to fill time. It's to hurt with it, then heal with it."

And then there is silence. Beginners fear it. It feels like failure, like dead space. Artists use it.

A pianist learning to improvise plays constantly, terrified of gaps. Every rest gets filled with another note, another flourish. The music is dense, busy, exhausting. Their teacher stops them. "Play less. Leave space. Let the silence do some of the work."

The silences feel like falling. But the pianist learns to remain inside the falling long enough to hear what silence does: how it creates anticipation, how it lets the previous phrase land, how it gives the listener time to feel what just happened.

The music transforms. Not because the pianist got better at playing. Because they got better at not playing.

Most cultures train urgency. Everything is faster, now, immediately, optimize. Art trains something else: the capacity to remain operative while the urgency persists. The artist learns to trust not-yet, almost, hold, release. Their nervous system lowers its compulsion to control time and begins to move with it.

•　　•　　•

Choosing Without Proof

Eventually, every artist reaches a moment that cannot be solved through logic, technique, or consensus.

A painting is technically perfect, every rule followed, every proportion correct, and dead. A poem follows every constraint of form, meter, rhyme, and structure intact, and says nothing. A scene hits every plot beat, setup, conflict, resolution, and misses the truth.

Skill without coherence is empty.

A photographer stands in a darkroom, looking at two prints of the same image. One is exposed slightly longer, shadows deeper, highlights more subdued. The other is brighter, clearer, easier to read. Both are technically sound. Both are beautiful in their way. But one is true. And the photographer knows it, not because they can explain it, not because anyone else would agree, but because when they look at the darker print, something in their chest opens. The image breathes. It feels inevitable.

They choose the darker print. They can't prove it's right. They just know.

Artists learn to detect falseness the way the body detects imbalance, not through evaluation but through registration. When the work is technically accomplished but emotionally dishonest. When the gesture is meant to impress rather than reveal. When something is real, even if it's strange, risky, raw, or breaks every convention. When something is false, the artist feels it as a held breath that won't release. When something is true, the breath comes back.

There is no proof that a brushstroke must be this way. There is no evidence that this cut is the only truthful one. There is no metric for whether a metaphor carries the weight of memory.

The artist must choose anyway.

A novelist writes two endings. One is satisfying, wraps up loose ends, gives the reader closure, feels complete. The other is devastating, leaves questions unanswered, honors ambiguity, and refuses to comfort. The novel wants the second ending. The novelist knows this. But they're terrified. Readers might hate it, agents might reject it, it violates expectations.

They choose the devastating ending. Because anything else would be a lie.

• • •

Revealing What Was Already There

When these capacities have matured, when the artist has learned to stay in the body, sense others, move with time, and choose through coherence, something extraordinary emerges.

The artist stops trying to impose meaning on the world. Instead, they begin to reveal meaning in the world.

Early in the journey, artists believe their job is to express themselves: to take what's inside and put it outside. But somewhere along the way, the relationship inverts. The work is no longer about the artist. It is about what the artist is able to see, hear, and reveal that others have missed.

A photographer walks through a city at dawn. Most people would see empty streets, closed shops, the ordinary architecture of a Tuesday morning. But the photographer sees the way light hits a fire escape at exactly this angle, creating shadows that look like prison bars. The exhaustion in the posture of a woman waiting for a bus. The tenderness in the graffiti someone spray-painted on a dumpster: "Still here. Still fighting."

The photographer doesn't invent these things. They were there all along. But they give them form, not to show off their vision, but to say: look. Can you feel that this is true?

A photograph does not invent tenderness. It catches the tenderness people have been too rushed or defended to see. A poem does not create longing. It grants longing a structure so it can be held. A film does not create loneliness. It gives loneliness a language. A dance does not manufacture grief. It lets grief move through bodies until it becomes witnessed, shared, human.

When art lands, when a painting stops you, when a song breaks you open, when a film stays with you for days, it is not because the artist told you something new. It is because they showed you something you already knew but could not name.

Because the artist didn't see inside them. The artist saw the world clearly, and in seeing it clearly, revealed what we all carry but can't articulate.

•   •   •

The Cost of Staying

If artistry were built only from these capacities, anyone could become an artist with enough time.

But thousands begin art. Hundreds continue. Very few stay long enough to be changed.

What separates the practitioner from the artist is not talent, inspiration, intelligence, or confidence. It is whether they cross the thresholds that hurt.

The work collapses. A painter spends six months on a series, dozens of canvases, a gallery show scheduled, and two weeks before the opening, sees the work clearly for the first time: it is empty. Technically competent. Emotionally fraudulent. They have two choices: show it anyway, or start over.

The artist cancels the show. Not dramatically. Not as a statement. Just quietly, because showing the work would be a lie.

And then there is nothing. No new direction. No clarity about what went wrong. No certainty that beginning again will produce anything better. Just the absence of the thing they spent six months building, and the knowledge that they are the one who destroyed it.

Every major breakthrough is preceded by a period like this: where nothing works, nothing makes sense, and the artist has no idea who they are anymore. The question is whether you can stay in that space long enough for something new to emerge.

Most people can't.

The judgment arrives. A young playwright has a reading of her first full-length play. She sits in the back of the room, heart pounding, as actors read her words aloud for the first time. The feedback is brutal. Half the people hate the ending. Someone calls the protagonist unlikable. Another says the dialogue feels forced.

She listens. She hears everything. She doesn't defend. She doesn't collapse.

Later, alone, she sits with it. Some of the feedback reveals blind spots she couldn't see. Some of it misses the point entirely. She cannot yet tell which is which. That takes days.

She revises, not to please them, but to honor what the play is trying to become.

And then there is the long middle. A novelist is three years into a book. The initial excitement is gone. No one is waiting for this book. No publisher has offered a contract. There is no guarantee anyone will ever read it.

They wake up at five in the morning anyway. They write. Not because it feels good. Not because they are motivated. But because not writing would be a kind of death.

•　　•　　•

What Survives the Crossing

Those who stay, who endure the collapse of the work, who create under judgment, who return without applause, emerge changed. Not better. Not superior. Different.

They carry a steadiness that is not rigidity but availability. A sensitivity to timing that cannot be taught in words. A capacity for coherence under pressure that has nothing to do with intelligence and everything to do with what their nervous system learned through sustained contact with demanding practice.

They have been dismantled by the work and reconstituted by it. They have lost their original relationship to certainty, to ego, to the need for external validation, and found something more durable in its place.

What remains is not confidence. Confidence is fragile. It depends on outcomes, on applause, on being right. What remains is something quieter: a practiced capacity to remain in contact with what is real, even when what is real is difficult, uncertain, or exposing. The artists we studied did not describe this as courage, though it looked like courage from the outside. They described it as the inability to lie, the recognition that protection would destroy the work. What fell away was not fear but the reflex to shield against it.

Art does not use courage. Art produces it.

$\bullet \qquad \bullet \qquad \bullet$

Across sixteen disciplines, across decades of research, across every difference of medium, culture, tradition, and personality, the same interior journey kept appearing.

The journey from person to practitioner to someone who has been fundamentally changed by what they practiced.

The body learns to stay. Attention learns to widen. Time learns to breathe. Judgment learns to trust what cannot be proven. And something in the artist's relationship to the world shifts: from imposing meaning to revealing it.

If this journey were idiosyncratic, if it appeared only in dancers, or only in painters, or only in a particular culture, it would be interesting but not consequential.

It appears everywhere.

Which means it is not about art. It is about what happens to a human being who stays in contact with a demanding practice long enough to be transformed by it.

The next chapter enters that transformation from the inside, not as theory, but as lived experience. One artist. One crucible. Five days until opening night. Everything breaking at once.

THREE
The Formation Gap

**What it costs to lead without what
was never built**

There is a kind of exhaustion that rest does not fix.

You have felt it. Not the tiredness that comes from long hours or difficult decisions or too many meetings. Something quieter. Something that accumulates in the space between what you are doing and who you are while doing it.

It shows up after the town hall that went well, technically. People asked questions. You answered them clearly. The slides were right, the message was right, the tone was right. And when you walked back to your office, something was wrong. Not in the room. In you. A hollowness that had nothing to do with what happened and everything to do with how you held yourself while it was happening.

It shows up in the meeting where everyone agrees and no one commits. The energy is flat. The words are correct. The nods come on time. And underneath it all, you can feel something withdrawing. The part of people that takes risks, tells difficult truths, and invests something personal. That part has already left the room. Everyone is still there. The thing that matters is gone.

It shows up in the decision that was right and still corroded trust. You weighed the options. You consulted the people who needed consulting. You made the call. It was defensible. It was necessary. And three months later, something between you and your team had thinned, not because the decision was wrong, but because of how it landed. How it felt to receive. What it signaled about what you were willing to see.

It shows up in the one-on-one with the person you are losing. They haven't said they're leaving. But you can feel it. Something in their posture, their pacing, the way they have stopped pushing back. You have five minutes to understand what is actually happening beneath the surface, and you realize, with a sinking clarity, that you do not have the instrument for this. You have tools for performance conversations. You do not have the capacity for this one.

It shows up in the moment after the crisis, when everyone is looking at you for what comes next. Not the plan. They know you'll have a plan. What they need is something harder to name. They need to feel, from you, that the ground has not disappeared. That what just happened can be survived. That the thing that holds the group together is still holding. And you realize that what they are asking for is not your expertise. It is your presence. And you are not sure you have it.

It shows up in the recognition, late at night or early in the morning, that you have been carrying something for a very long time and you do not know how to set it down. Not the work itself. The weight of how you hold yourself while doing the work. The constant calibration: how much to show, how much to absorb, when to speak, when to stay silent, how to project what the room needs without losing yourself inside the projection.

It shows up the next day. And the day after that.

The same meeting with different people. The same steadiness performed for a different audience. The same careful modulation of voice and posture and eye contact. You walk into the room already preparing how you will stand. You leave the room already replaying what you said. In between, you are not quite present, not fully absent either, but operating from a place that is slightly removed from what is happening, watching yourself hold the space while the space asks for something you are not sure you have.

It shows up in the drive home, or the walk to the train, or the fifteen minutes you sit in the car before going inside. You are not processing anything specific. You are metabolizing the residue of being watched. The aftertaste of rooms where you were the person everyone looked to, and where what they needed from you was not your expertise but your composure, your groundedness, your willingness to absorb what they could not hold.

It shows up in the moment when someone asks how you are and you say "fine," not because you are lying, but because the truth is too diffuse to articulate. You are not burned out. You are not depressed. You are not failing. You are managing. You are compensating. You are doing the work and doing it well.

And something inside you is slowly, quietly, becoming less available.

Monday arrives and it is the same as the last one. The calendar is full. The decisions are waiting. The rooms will need holding. You prepare, not the content, you already know the content, you prepare yourself. How you will enter. What you will project.

Where you will sit so the light is right, so the angle communicates authority without distance, openness without vulnerability. You have been doing this so long that it is automatic. You no longer notice the preparation. You only notice the tiredness afterward, the specific tiredness that comes not from the work but from the effort of being a particular kind of person while doing it.

And on Thursday, or Friday, or the Sunday before it starts again, you sit with something you cannot name. It is not dread exactly. It is not boredom. It is closer to depletion, but not the kind rest fixes. It is the depletion of having been somebody for five days straight. Of having held a shape. Of having been the leader the room needed while the person inside that leader waited, patient and unseen, for a moment that never came.

Leaders do not often speak about these moments. Not because they lack the language. Because the language they have, alignment, engagement, communication, execution, does not reach where they are actually standing.

•   •   •

Why Skill Isn't Failing

This is not a failure of preparation.

The leaders who feel this are not incompetent. They are often the most prepared people in the room. They have read the research. They have invested in coaching. They understand emotional intelligence, psychological safety, adaptive leadership, and systems thinking. They can name what good leadership looks like.

And still, in the live moment, when the room goes tense, when the question has no good answer, when the person across from them needs something that information cannot provide, something is missing.

Not knowledge. Not skill. Not effort.

The missing thing is harder to name because it is not a thing at all. It is a way of being. A quality of presence that allows the leader to remain steady when steadiness is what the room needs most. A capacity to hold what is happening without rushing to fix it, explain it, or escape it.

Skills execute. They give you something to do when the moment arrives. And there are moments where doing is exactly right, where the situation calls for a decision, a plan, a clear directive.

But there are other moments, and they are the moments that define leadership, where doing is not what is needed. Where the room does not need your plan. It needs your presence. Where the person across from you does not need your answer. They need to feel that you are actually there. Where the team does not need another communication about the strategy. They need to see someone standing in the uncertainty with them who is not pretending it isn't there.

You know these moments because they feel different in your body. The competence moments feel solvable: there is a problem, a tool, an action. The formation moments feel different. They feel like standing at an edge. Like being asked for something that cannot be produced on demand. Like the gap between what you have and what the moment requires is not a gap of knowledge but a gap of being.

In the competence moments, you know what to do, and you do it.

In the formation moments, you know what is needed, and you cannot become it.

Not because you are unwilling. Because becoming is not something you can decide to do in the moment. Becoming happens before the moment arrives, through years of contact with a practice that gradually reshapes how you inhabit pressure, silence, exposure, and uncertainty. If that contact never happened, the moment finds you as you are: competent, prepared, and not yet formed for what the room is asking.

This is what it feels like in the body: a slight vertigo. A sense of reaching for something that is not there. You have the knowledge. You have the language. You have the intention. And underneath all of it, you can feel the absence of ground, the specific absence of a self that has been built for this, that has practiced this, that can meet this moment not from effort but from formation.

These moments cannot be met with more preparation. They can only be met with a kind of readiness that lives deeper than skill: in the body, in the nervous system, in the practiced capacity to stay when everything in you wants to retreat.

Most leadership development builds competence. Almost none builds formation.

•   •   •

Performance Without Ground

If you have led long enough, you know what it feels like to perform steadiness you do not feel.

To walk into a room after receiving news that changes everything, and project calm. To stand before a team that is afraid and offer confidence you have not yet found in yourself. To hold your voice level when your chest is tight, your breath is shallow, and your mind is racing through scenarios, none of which are good.

Notice what happens in your body when you imagine this. Maybe your shoulders lift slightly. Maybe your jaw tightens. Maybe your breathing changes. The breath that was moving freely a moment ago now takes a shorter path, staying high in the chest, not reaching the belly. This is the body's preparation for performance. You have done it a thousand times. It is so habitual that you may not even notice it anymore.

But your team notices. Not consciously. They cannot say what they see. But something in them registers the difference between a leader who is present and a leader who is performing presence. The shoulders that are held rather than settled. The voice that is controlled rather than grounded. The eye contact that is steady because it is managed, not because the person behind it is actually there.

The body tells the truth before the mind can intervene. This is why the performance is so exhausting: it requires overriding the body's honest signals with manufactured ones, continuously, for hours, in rooms where the stakes are real and the scrutiny is constant.

Your voice learns to flatten. Not because you intend it to, but because modulation becomes management. The voice that once rose and fell with genuine feeling becomes a tool: calibrated for reassurance, for gravity, for control. You hear yourself speak in meetings and the sound is correct but the texture is thin. The warmth is performed. The steadiness is held in place by tension, not by ground. You are producing the sounds of presence without the felt experience of being present.

Your shoulders carry what your words do not. The tension that cannot be spoken settles there: between the shoulder blades, at the base of the neck, in the jaw that tightens before you walk into the room and does not fully release until you walk out. The body is keeping count of what the mind refuses to tally: the number of times you absorbed someone else's anxiety, the moments you swallowed your own uncertainty, the cost of every smile that was strategic rather than genuine.

Over time, this accumulates. Not as injury. As weight. The weight of a body that has been asked to perform coherence it was never given a way to build. The weight of a nervous system running in override mode so consistently that override becomes its resting state.

Leaders do this every day. They metabolize anxiety so their teams don't have to. They absorb the emotional temperature of the room and try to regulate it through their own composure. They perform presence.

But performance without ground is not sustainable.

When a leader performs composure without having built the interior capacity for it, the performance hollows them out. Each time they project confidence they do not possess, something thins. Each time they absorb the room's anxiety without having a practiced way to metabolize it, the anxiety accumulates, not in the team, but in the leader's body. Each time they stand in front of people and offer steadiness that is manufactured rather than formed, the distance between who they are and who they are performing widens.

At first, the distance is small. You barely notice it. You tell yourself this is just part of the role that every leader performs, that composure is a skill like any other. And in a sense, it is. But over months and years, the distance becomes structural. The performance calcifies into habit. The habit becomes the identity. And one day, you realize you cannot remember the last time you were fully present in a room without calculating how to appear.

You can see it in leaders who are admired and exhausted. Who are effective and quietly eroding. Who hold the organization together while something inside them comes apart.

The private suffering of leaders is not weakness. It is the predictable consequence of asking people to carry emotional, symbolic, and relational responsibilities they were never trained to hold.

•　　•　　•

There is a meeting you remember.

Not the details. The details have faded. You remember the room. The light. The quality of silence before it started. You were already tired when you walked in. Not the kind of tired you mention. The other kind.

People were seated. You took your chair. Someone was presenting: numbers, timelines, the language of progress. You listened. You nodded at the right moments. You asked a question that showed you were tracking. You did everything the room expected.

And then something shifted. Not in the room. In you.

It was subtle. A feeling of distance. As though you had stepped back from yourself by an inch. You were still speaking. Still engaging. But the part of you that meant it had gone quiet. You could feel the gap between the words you were producing and whatever was actually happening inside you. The words were professional. What was happening inside you had no name.

Someone asked you a direct question. You paused. Not because you didn't know the answer. Because for a moment, you could not find the self that answers questions. The competent self. The grounded self. The self that holds rooms. It was there, it is always there, but you had to reach for it, and the reaching felt further than usual.

You answered. The answer was fine. No one noticed.

The meeting continued. You continued inside it. But something had opened that you could not close. An awareness of the effort. Not the effort of the work, the effort of being the person doing the work. The effort of producing coherence in real time, from a place inside you that felt less like ground and more like habit.

Afterward, you sat for a moment. You did not check your phone. You did not stand up immediately. You sat.

Something was trying to surface. You could feel it the way you feel a word you've forgotten: present but unreachable. Not a thought. A recognition. That this, what had just happened in that room, was not an aberration. It was not a bad day. It was the texture of your leadership most days. The slight distance. The manufactured engagement. The performance that passes for presence because no one in the room knows the difference. Including, most of the time, you.

You sat a moment longer. Then you stood, and walked into the next room, and began again.

•　　•　　•

What Happens When Formation Is Missing

The consequences are not dramatic. They are erosive.

They happen in rooms where everything looks fine.

Trust thins without conflict. No one did anything wrong. No promise was broken. But over time, the quality of connection between a leader and their team degrades, not because of betrayal, but because the leader's presence stopped landing. They were there in body. They were not there in a way people could feel. And trust, it turns out, is not built on reliability alone. It is built on the felt sense that the person in front of you is actually present to what is happening.

When that presence is performed rather than real, people sense it. They may not name it. But they adjust. They pull back. They stop bringing the difficult things. They stop arguing, not because they agree, but because disagreement requires trust, and trust requires feeling that the other person is actually in the room with you. Not managing the room. In it.

The leader notices the silence and interprets it as alignment. It is not alignment. It is withdrawal. And the distance grows.

Meaning erodes without failure. The work continues. Targets are met. Quarters close. But somewhere along the way, the sense that the work matters, that it connects to something larger than the metric, quietly disappears. Not because someone took it away. Because no one is making it. People do the work. They do not give themselves to it. They show up, perform competence, and leave with nothing to carry them into the next day except the obligation to return.

You can feel this in organizations. The meetings that are efficient and dead. The updates that are accurate and meaningless. The goals that are clear and uninspiring. Everything is working. Nothing is alive.

Ethical drift occurs without intent.

The leader who has no practiced way to sit with moral complexity begins to simplify it. The decision that should have been held longer gets made too quickly because the discomfort of not knowing is intolerable. The conversation that should have happened doesn't because the leader cannot hold the relational weight of it. The boundary that should have been drawn isn't because drawing it requires a kind of presence, a willingness to be visible in the act of choosing, that the leader has never been formed to sustain.

No one intended to drift. But the capacity to stay was never built. And so the drift happens in the spaces where staying was required: in the pause before the decision, in the silence after the hard question, in the moment when the right thing to do was clear, and the cost of doing it felt unbearable. The leader moved past those moments. Not maliciously. Not even consciously. They simply did not have the practiced capacity to hold still in them long enough for something honest to emerge.

Identity fractures under pressure. This is the deepest cost and the least discussed.

Leaders who spend years performing a self they have not been formed into eventually lose contact with the self underneath. The role consumes the person. The performance becomes the identity. And when the performance is disrupted, by failure, by crisis, by the kind of moment that strips away everything that isn't real, there is nothing beneath it to stand on. This is not a failure of character. It is the absence of formation.

The thinning happens in small ways first. You notice that your range has narrowed. The humor that used to surface in difficult moments: gone. The spontaneity that once allowed you to say the unexpected thing, the honest thing, the thing that broke the tension and let people breathe: gone. You have become careful. Measured. Appropriate. Every response runs through an internal filter: How will this land? What will they read into it? Am I projecting the right thing?

You stop saying what you think and start saying what is strategic. You stop responding to what you feel and start responding to what is expected. The gap is invisible to everyone else. You are still effective. You are still admired. But the person who used to surprise themselves has been replaced by someone who manages the impression they make. And the managing never stops.

There is a grief in this, but it never quite arrives. It stays at the periphery: a vague sense of loss without an object. You cannot grieve a self you are still performing. You cannot mourn a spontaneity you are still successfully containing. The loss is real and unnamed, and because it is unnamed, it registers as exhaustion, as cynicism, as the slow conviction that this is simply what senior leadership costs.

Some leaders learn to live inside this thinning indefinitely. They become highly functional, well-regarded, and quietly hollow. They lead from the outside of themselves. The work gets done. The results come in. And something that was once alive in them has become a function.

It is only in the rare, unguarded moment, usually after something breaks, that the leader sees it clearly.

Maybe it is a health scare. Maybe it is a public failure. Maybe it is the quiet implosion of a relationship that could not survive the distance between the role and the person. Maybe it is just a Tuesday afternoon when the performance briefly fails, when you are sitting in a meeting, and you suddenly cannot do it, cannot produce the composure, cannot find the projected self, and for a moment, the room sees you. Actually sees you. And instead of the disaster you expected, something shifts. People lean in. People soften. The conversation becomes real in a way it has not been in months.

And in that moment, you understand: the thing that was missing was not more skill. It was you. Your actual presence. The self you have been protecting by performing a different one.

You understand, in a flash, that you may not be able to hold, you have been trying to meet formation demands with competence tools. You have been asked to hold what can only be held by someone who has been changed by practice, and you have been trying to hold it with skill, with strategy, with will.

And will, no matter how strong, is not the same as formation.

Will fatigues. Formation endures.

The Developmental Void

Consider what happens when a promising manager is promoted into a senior leadership role.

They are given training in strategic thinking, performance management, communication skills, and emotional intelligence. They learn frameworks for decision-making, models for motivation, and tools for delegation. All of this is valuable.

But none of it prepares them for the experience of being watched. Of having every gesture, every tone, every silence interpreted as a signal. None of it trains them for the weight of knowing their decisions will affect people's livelihoods, identities, and futures. None of it builds the capacity to hold steady when they themselves are uncertain, afraid, or overwhelmed.

In the first year, they compensate with energy. They work harder. They prepare more thoroughly. They arrive earlier and stay later. They study the people around them and try to understand what is expected. This works for a while, the effort masks the absence. The preparation substitutes for presence. The long hours create the illusion of groundedness.

But the moments keep arriving. The room that needs holding. The silence that needs to be met without filling. The person who needs to feel that their leader is actually seeing them. And each time, the leader reaches for what they have, knowledge, skill, strategy, will, and each time, the moment asks for something else. Something that cannot be produced. Something that had to have been built before the moment arrived.

Where is the developmental lineage for this?

Where is the apprenticeship in presence under pressure?

Where is the training in reading the emotional field of a room, not analyzing it after the fact, but sensing it in real time, in the body, while the meeting is still unfolding? Where is the practice in knowing intuitively what will land and what will fragment? Where is the cultivation of the capacity to hold moral complexity without collapsing into certainty?

And so leaders improvise. They draw on whatever they have, personality, instinct, fragments of experience, and try to meet moments they were never developed for. Some manage. Some even thrive. But they do it without a lineage, without a developmental pathway, without the benefit of centuries of refined practice in the very capacities the role demands.

This is the loneliness that leadership language cannot reach. Not the loneliness of decision-making or authority. The loneliness of having no tradition to draw from when the moment asks you to be more than you have been trained to be. The loneliness of knowing that what you need is not another tool or framework, but a fundamentally different kind of preparation: one that would have changed not what you know but who you are.

They are performing without rehearsal. Making meaning without training in meaning-making. Holding rooms without having been held inside a practice that teaches you how.

And somewhere, in the background of all of this, beneath the coping and the competence and the quiet exhaustion, a question begins to form. Not a strategic question. Not a question about skills or development or the next program to attend. Something more unsettling.

It is the sense that what you need is not more of what you already have. That the gap is not a gap of knowledge or even of skill. That no amount of learning will close it, because it is not a learning gap. It is a formation gap. Something in you was supposed to have been built, slowly, through contact with a practice that demanded you change, and it was not. And you have been compensating for its absence with effort and intelligence and will for so long that the compensating has become invisible to you.

You may not be able to articulate this. But your body knows it. Your fatigue knows it. The distance between your role and your self knows it.

•   •   •

I know this because I lived it.

I was on page thirty of a manuscript I was not sure would become anything. I had left my career to write one book. I didn't want to leave this world without having done that. I was living on savings, researching, writing, starting over, researching again. The work was slow and uncertain, and I honored it anyway, not because I believed it would succeed but because something in the practice itself was asking me to stay.

It was too much. I took a job. The job led to a second job. I was a CEO of one company, a director of another. I was good at both. I held rooms. I made decisions. I projected the composure people needed. And each day, something in me died a little. Not because the work was bad. Because I had been inside something that was forming me, and I had walked away from it, and the walking away felt like the responsible thing and also like a slow surrender.

Six months in, I quit the CEO role. I leaned back into the writing. I finished the book. I published it. And then I wrote another, and another, and never looked back.

The formation gap is not a theory I arrived at through research. It is a distance I carried in my body for six months: the distance between the leader I was performing and the writer who had been on page thirty, waiting for me to come back and finish what the practice had started.

•   •   •

If leadership requires capacities that only emerge through formation, through sustained, embodied practice under constraint that changes not what you know but who you are under pressure, where has that formation been happening?

Not in business schools. Not in executive programs. Not in coaching certifications, competency frameworks, or leadership retreats.

Not in any discipline that calls itself leadership.

Somewhere else. Quietly. For centuries.

FOUR

The Lineage No One Claimed

**How a parallel human technology of formation
evolved, because the work demanded it**

There are forms of human work where judgment must be exercised before certainty arrives.

Where the person acting cannot wait for proof, consensus, or permission, because the moment will not wait. Where the quality of what happens depends not on what the person knows but on who they have become. Where rules are insufficient, planning is inadequate, and the only thing that determines whether the moment holds or collapses is the practiced capacity of the person standing inside it.

You have felt this. Not as abstraction. In the room where a question was asked and the silence that followed was not empty but full, full of consequence, full of the room's attention pressing against you, full of the knowledge that what you said next would shape what people believed about themselves and their situation. In that silence, you could not calculate your way to the right answer. You could only meet the moment with whatever you had available, and whatever you had available was not a plan. It was you.

This constraint has always existed. In every era, in every culture, there have been moments that demanded presence before proof, meaning before consensus, coherence before certainty. The healer deciding which remedy to offer before the diagnosis was clear, reading the patient's color, their breathing, the quality of their fear, and making a judgment that could not be justified by evidence but must be justified by the outcome. The elder speaking to the community after disaster, shaping what the crisis meant before the facts were fully known, knowing that the story told in the first hours would become the story that held. The navigator reading the sea's mood before the storm had announced itself, sensing from the swell, the wind, the color of the horizon, that the moment to change course was now, not after the weather confirmed it.

The question has always been the same: what kind of human being can meet this constraint without breaking?

And beneath that question, a harder one: how do you build such a person?

Not through instruction. Instruction prepares you for what is known. This pressure lives where the known runs out. Not through willpower. Will can hold for a day, a week, a crisis, but the demand does not relent. It arrives again tomorrow, and the day after, and the year after that. What is needed is not effort but capacity. Not performance but formation. Something that has been built into the person so deeply that it does not require summoning. That is simply there when the moment demands it.

Leadership faces this constraint now. It did not always. For most of a century, leadership could operate inside systems stable enough that certainty arrived before judgment was required. Plans could be made. Answers could be found. The rules, while imperfect, were sufficient. Leaders could prepare, execute, and review, and the gap between what they faced and what they had available to offer was manageable. Uncomfortable, sometimes. But manageable.

That world is gone.

And in its absence, leaders face the oldest constraint in human work, the one that was never new, only newly inescapable: act before you know. Hold before you understand. Be present to what is happening when what is happening has no name yet.

Somewhere, a lineage of practice evolved to meet this demand. Not because the practitioners were wise or virtuous. Because the work required it.

•　　•　　•

Once you know what to look for, you see it everywhere.

In the conductor who walks to the podium and does not raise the baton immediately. Who stands in the silence, letting the orchestra's collective attention settle, reading the room's energy before giving it shape. Watch the conductor's hands. They are not still, they are listening. Something in the fingers is sensing the room the way a physician's hand reads a pulse. The conductor cannot know what the performance will be. It has not happened yet. Every night is different: the humidity in the hall, the fatigue in the brass section, the restlessness of the audience. There is no data to consult. There is no algorithm that predicts what this particular room needs from this particular downbeat on this particular night. The conductor must judge before certainty arrives. Must act from presence, not from plan. Must offer coherence to eighty musicians who are waiting for a signal that is not merely technical but felt.

And here is the thing most people miss: the conductor's capacity to do this is not talent. It was built. Through years of standing in front of ensembles and getting it wrong, giving a downbeat that was too sharp, too soft, too eager, too cautious, and learning, in the body, not in the mind, what the room needed. Through thousands of rehearsals where the pressure appeared in small form: this passage is not working, the tempo is technically correct, but the phrasing is dead, something must change, and the change cannot be specified, only sensed. The conductor was formed by sustained contact with a demand that never relented: judge now, with incomplete information, under exposure, and live with the consequences.

In the theater director who watches a dress rehearsal and knows, without being able to explain it, that the second act is false. Not technically wrong, the blocking is correct, the lines are memorized, the transitions are clean. But something is dishonest. Something in the actors' bodies is held rather than inhabited. The director has no metric for this. No instrument. Only a judgment refined over years of watching human beings under the pressure of exposure, years of learning to see the difference between someone who is performing truth and someone who is standing inside it.

The director makes a single adjustment. Not a note about performance, a question about truth. "What are you protecting yourself from in this scene?" The actor pauses. The room goes quiet. And when the scene runs again, something has shifted that no technical direction could have produced. The dishonesty is gone. What replaced it cannot be named, only felt. The audience, when they see this scene, will not know what the director did. They will only know that the scene is true.

In the ceramicist who studies a crack in the glaze and must decide, now, whether it is a flaw to be corrected or a threshold the piece needed to cross. In the jazz pianist who plays the wrong chord and must decide, in this beat, whether to retreat to safety or build from the rupture. In the photographer who has been waiting for hours and must decide, in this fraction of a second, that the moment has arrived, that the light and the subject and the meaning have converged into something that will not happen again.

Each time, the same demand: judgment before certainty. Presence under exposure. Coherence offered from a place that cannot be manufactured in the moment but must have been formed before the moment arrived.

What you are seeing is not talent. Not creativity. Not self-expression. You are seeing the result of formation.

A human being who has been changed by sustained contact with this pressure until their capacity to meet it became structural. Not effortful. Not performed. Built.

•　　•　　•

There is a misunderstanding so deep it has become invisible.

Art, in the popular imagination, is expression. It is what people do when they have something inside them that needs to come out. It is creativity, inspiration, the province of the gifted and the eccentric. It is optional, beautiful, perhaps moving, but ultimately separate from the serious work of holding organizations, making decisions, and leading people through difficulty.

This misunderstanding has kept an entire formation lineage outside the reach of the people who need it most.

Because the misunderstanding is not about art's value. It is about art's function. As long as artistry is understood as expression, as what happens when gifted people release their inner vision, it remains culturally admired and structurally irrelevant. Something to appreciate. Not something to learn from. Certainly not something that has been quietly solving the exact problem leadership now faces.

The truth is simpler and more devastating: art was not built to express. Art was built to hold.

To form. To produce human beings who could do what no amount of knowledge, planning, or willpower could do alone, stand inside the constraint and meet it with coherence.

The disciplines that carry this lineage today, dance, music, theater, visual arts, poetry, film, sculpture, and improvisation, are the inheritors of something ancient and functional. Each one preserves, in its training practices and performance traditions, a refined method for forming human beings who can hold meaning under pressure, stay present under exposure, sense what a situation needs, and offer coherence when coherence has broken down.

This is not what we usually mean when we say "art." But it is what art has always been for.

What the Constraint Demanded

The constraint never went away. That is the first thing to understand.

In every artistic discipline, the practitioner faces the same irreducible pressure: the work must be done under conditions of exposure, uncertainty, and consequence, and it must be done now. Not after more preparation. Not after the answer becomes clear. Now. In front of people. With no guarantee that what emerges will be coherent, true, or enough.

The painter faces it every time the brush touches the canvas. There is no undo. The stroke either serves the painting or it doesn't, and the painter must judge in the moment of contact, not afterward. The dancer faces it every time the music begins. The body must respond, not from thought but from a readiness that is either present or absent, that was either built through years of practice or was not. The poet faces it in the silence before the line arrives, when the pressure to fill the page with something adequate competes with the deeper knowledge that adequacy is not enough, that the line must be true or the poem will fail.

And because this pressure never went away, the disciplines that lived under it had to evolve practices that could form human beings to survive it. Not to endure it temporarily. To survive it as a way of life.

Consider what this actually asks of the body. It asks for exposure: the willingness to be seen, judged, and held accountable for what you produce, without the armor of anonymity or the safety of revision. The painter's canvas hangs on a wall for strangers to judge. The actor stands on a stage with nowhere to hide. The musician performs in real time, and what emerges cannot be taken back. Every artistic discipline assumes that the practitioner will be exposed and trains them to stay inside that exposure rather than defend against it.

It asks for failure, not as exception but as method. The rehearsal room is built for failure. The studio assumes that most of what is made will be discarded. The practice room assumes that mastery emerges through ten thousand repetitions, most of which are inadequate. Failure is not the interruption of artistic training. It is the curriculum.

It asks for identity risk, the acceptance that the work will change the maker. A serious artistic practice does not leave the practitioner's identity intact. The dancer's body is remade. The actor's emotional range is broken open. The writer's certainties are dissolved by what the story needs to say. Artistic formation is not additive. It is erosive before it is constructive.

Not to endure it through will. Will fatigues, we have already seen this in leaders who perform composure until the performance hollows them out. What was needed ran deeper: practices that could reshape the practitioner's nervous system, their relationship to uncertainty, their capacity for exposure, their tolerance for ambiguity, their judgment under pressure, so that when the moment arrived, they could meet it from formation rather than from effort.

This is what art was actually built to do. Not to express. Not to beautify. Not to entertain. To form human beings who could hold judgment, meaning, and presence under conditions that could not be resolved by rules, speed, or certainty.

Long before art became a cultural category, it existed to do this work. Think of the storyteller in any ancient tradition. They did not simply recite events. They held a room. They read the listeners' readiness, the grief that needed naming, the fear that needed containing, the hope that needed permission to surface. They paced the telling to the collective breath of the group. They knew when to pause, not for dramatic effect, but because the silence was where the meaning actually lived. They carried, in their body and their voice and their practiced attention, a capacity that the community could not afford to lose.

And when the storyteller failed, when they misjudged the room, or told the wrong story, or rushed past the silence that needed holding, the community felt it. Not as aesthetic disappointment. As loss of coherence. The crisis that should have been held was instead amplified. The grief that should have been given form remained formless, and the formlessness corroded the bonds that held people together. The failure was not artistic. It was structural. The community needed someone formed for this work, and the person who stood before them was not yet formed enough.

These were not aesthetic luxuries. These were survival technologies. A community that could not hold meaning through crisis did not survive the crisis. A people that could not give form to what they feared and what they hoped lost the coherence that held them together. A tradition that could not train judgment beyond rules could not adapt when the rules stopped working.

Art evolved because human communities needed people who could hold what could not be held through logic, planning, or force. And the only way to produce such people was through practices that exposed them, repeatedly, to the demand itself, until their capacity to meet it became part of who they were.

Not a skill they possessed. A quality of being they had become.

This is the formation logic that artistry carries. It did not evolve from theory. It evolved from necessity, from the irreducible fact that the work demanded people who were formed for it, and no other method of formation worked.

· · ·

How the Practices Evolved

The constraint shaped the practices. Not the other way around.

Because the work demanded judgment before certainty, the practices had to train judgment without rules. The rehearsal room evolved, not as a place to perfect what was already known, but as a place to encounter what could not yet be done.

Walk into any serious rehearsal space and you will feel it immediately. The room does not accommodate comfort. The mirrors reflect what you would rather not see. The floor is hard under the body. The light is unforgiving. And the director or teacher is watching, not for success, not even for progress, but for truth. For the moment when the practitioner stops performing and starts actually being present in the work.

This is what the practitioner experiences: the rehearsal strips away every habitual response. Every clever solution, every performative gesture, every way of appearing competent without being present, the rehearsal finds it and makes it visible. What remains is the gap between what the practitioner can do and what the work requires. That gap is not a problem to be solved. It is the space where formation happens. The practitioner stays inside it, day after day, week after week, and something in them begins to change. Not their knowledge. Their capacity.

Because the work demanded presence under exposure, the practices had to train the practitioner's nervous system to stay rather than flee. Critique evolved, not evaluation that judges outcomes, but critique that forms the maker.

In a serious studio critique, the work is placed before others and examined. Not for whether it is good or bad, but for whether it is honest. Whether the maker is present in it. Whether the choices reflect coherence or avoidance. The practitioner sits and listens. Their hands may tremble slightly. Their stomach tightens. Every instinct says defend, explain, justify. But the practice demands a different response: hear it. Absorb it. Do not collapse. Do not armor. And then return to the work, changed by what was seen. This is exposure, judgment, and consequence appearing in concentrated form. The practitioner crosses this threshold so many times that crossing becomes capacity.

Because the work demanded coherence without certainty, the practices had to train the practitioner to create from what is, not from what is planned. Repetition evolved, not as rote, but as deepening. The pianist plays the same passage a hundred times, not to memorize it but to discover what lives inside it. Each repetition strips away one more layer of control, one more layer of habit, until what remains is the passage itself, played not from the pianist's effort but from the pianist's formation. The body knows. The mind gets out of the way. And what the body knows is not the notes, the notes were learned in the first five repetitions. What the body knows, after a hundred, is how to be present to the music without managing it.

Constraint evolved alongside repetition, the sonnet's fourteen lines, the stage's fixed dimensions, the budget's limits, the ensemble's size. Artistic disciplines do not treat constraints as obstacles. They treat them as crucibles. The pressure that forces the practitioner to find what they would never have discovered in freedom. The ceramicist working with a cracked kiln. The playwright working with four actors when the story wants ten. The filmmaker who has three minutes of screen time to make the audience understand a character's entire interior world. Each limit is the same pressure in a different form: you cannot have what you want. What will you make from what you have?

Because the work demanded meaning without proof, the practices had to train the practitioner to sustain silence. Silence evolved as practice, the pause between movements, the rest between notes, the empty space on the canvas. The compulsion to fill, to fix, to act is resisted. And what emerges from that resistance is often more true than what would have emerged from effort. The sculptor who stops carving and waits. The writer who puts down the pen and sits with the emptiness of the page. The musician who holds the rest longer than the audience expects, and in that held silence, something in the room changes. Attention deepens. The next note, when it comes, carries weight it could not have carried without the silence that preceded it.

Beneath all of these practices: a single formation logic, different from the logic of instruction.

Instruction says: here is what you need to know. Formation says: here is what you must go through. Instruction transfers knowledge. Formation transforms the knower. Instruction can be completed. Formation only deepens.

Every serious artistic tradition embeds this logic, not as theory but as structure. The practitioner does not learn formation as a concept. They undergo it as a process. And what they become on the other side is not someone who knows more. It is someone who can hold more, under exactly the conditions the work demands.

·　　·　　·

Why the Lineage Stayed Invisible

If this lineage has been forming human beings for these conditions for centuries, why did leadership never notice?

Because the constraint looked different from the outside.

When leadership scholars looked at artistic practice, they saw expression. They saw creativity. They saw talent, personality, aesthetic sensibility, interesting qualities, perhaps, but not transferable capacities. They did not see formation because formation does not announce itself. It lives inside the structure of the practice, invisible to anyone who has not undergone it. You cannot see what the rehearsal room does by watching a performance. You cannot see what critique builds by reading a review. You cannot see the years of threshold-crossing that produced the conductor's stillness by admiring the concert.

The prestige systems were different. Leadership scholarship drew from psychology, management science, and organizational behavior, disciplines with clear empirical methods, peer-reviewed journals, and institutional authority. Artistic practice drew from studios, rehearsal rooms, and master-apprentice traditions, lineages with deep wisdom but no peer-reviewed evidence base. In the academy that shaped leadership theory, artistic knowledge registered as intuition, not as knowledge.

The timeframes were different. Leadership development operates on compressed cycles, workshops, retreats, quarterly goals, and annual reviews. Results are expected in weeks. Impact is measured in months. Artistic formation operates on years. A dancer trains for a decade before their body can do what the choreography requires. A writer produces a million words before producing one that matters. Leadership's timeframe could not accommodate formation's pace. And so formation's outputs, steady presence, refined judgment, embodied coherence, were attributed to personality rather than practice. To who someone was rather than what they had undergone.

The relationship to failure was different. Leadership treats failure as deviation, something to be analyzed, corrected, and prevented. Artistic practice treats failure as formation, the necessary collapse that precedes every meaningful breakthrough. The dancer who falls. The actor who loses the scene. The writer who produces five hundred pages and throws them away. These are not deviations. They are the practice working as designed.

And the language was different.

Artistry speaks of presence, coherence, honesty, truth, exposure, staying, returning. Leadership speaks of alignment, execution, engagement, strategy, competence, and performance.

The two vocabularies describe overlapping realities but share almost no words.

Imagine a conductor and a CEO sitting across from each other, each describing what they do in the most critical moments of their work. The conductor would speak of listening, of sensing the ensemble's collective readiness, of holding tension until it resolves itself, of knowing when to lead the orchestra and when to follow the music's own momentum. Of feeling, in the body, when the second violins are rushing because they are anxious, and adjusting not the tempo but the quality of attention in the room.

The CEO would speak of aligning stakeholders, driving execution, managing change, and communicating vision. Of quarterly targets and strategic pivots and employee engagement scores.

They would each nod politely. They would each assume the other's work was interesting but fundamentally different from their own.

And they would both be wrong. Because the constraint underneath is the same: judgment before certainty, presence under exposure, coherence when the ground shifts. The capacities are the same. The formation is the same. But because the words never matched, the lineage never transferred. Each domain held half of what leaders need, and neither could see what the other carried.

•   •   •

This is not an argument that leaders should become artists. Artistic mastery and leadership mastery are not the same thing. A leader does not need to paint to cultivate judgment. Does not need to dance to develop presence. Does not need to perform on stage to learn what exposure teaches.

This is a claim about lineage.

Somewhere in human history, practices evolved that could form people for the oldest constraint in human work: the demand to hold judgment, meaning, and presence under conditions that cannot be resolved by rules, speed, or certainty. Those practices were embodied, repeated, threshold-crossing, identity-reshaping. They demanded that the practitioner change, not their strategy, but themselves. And they produced, over centuries of refinement, human beings who could hold what most people cannot.

Leadership never inherited this lineage. Not because it was unavailable. Because it was unrecognizable. Because the words were different. Because the timeframes were different. Because the measures of value were different. Because formation looks like nothing from the outside, until you need it, and it is either there or it is not.

It is recognizable now.

The constraint has not changed. Judgment before certainty. Presence under exposure. Meaning when the ground shifts. What has changed is that leadership can no longer avoid it. And what has always been true is now inescapable: a lineage of practice exists that was built for this. It was refined over centuries. It is still alive.

What remains is to enter that lineage from the inside.

FIVE

What You Already Recognize

The capacities that have no names yet

You already know when someone walks into a room and the room changes.

Not because of what they say. Before they say anything. Something in their body communicates what their words have not yet reached. The room adjusts. Shoulders drop. Breathing shifts. Attention gathers differently. You have felt this happen; sometimes you have been the one who caused it, and you could not explain how. You only knew that the room was different after you entered it, and you knew that the difference was not strategic. It was not planned. It came from somewhere in you that had no name.

You know when to stay silent.

Not the strategic silence of withholding information. The other kind. The kind where you feel the room holding something that cannot yet be spoken, and your body tells you, not your mind, your body, that words right now would break it. That the silence is doing work no sentence could do. You have sat inside that silence and felt the pressure to fill it, and sometimes you filled it and knew immediately that you should not have. And sometimes you held it, and something emerged from the group that could not have emerged if you had spoken. You could not explain afterward what you did. You did not do anything. You stayed.

You know the difference between a meeting that moved and a meeting that merely concluded.

The agenda was covered in both. The decisions were made in both. But in one of them, something happened between people that left them different from how they arrived. They leaned in. They said things they had not planned to say. The energy in the room gathered rather than scattered. And in the other meeting, the one that merely concluded, everything was correct, and nothing was alive. You could feel the difference. You could not name it.

You know when you are performing leadership and when you are actually leading.

The performance looks identical from the outside. The words are the same. The posture is confident. The decisions are sound. But inside, you can feel the gap, the distance between what you are projecting and what you are actually experiencing. And you know, though no one has ever taught you the vocabulary for this, that the people in the room can feel the gap too. They may not be able to name it. But their bodies register it. Their trust adjusts accordingly.

You know when timing matters more than content.

The same feedback delivered on Monday would have landed differently than it did on Thursday. The same announcement offered before the quarter ended would have meant something different than after. You have felt moments where the timing was right, where you said the thing at precisely the moment the room could receive it, and the words carried weight they would not have carried an hour earlier. You have also felt moments where the timing was wrong, and the words, however true, landed as noise.

None of this was taught to you.

Not in business school. Not in leadership development. Not in any workshop, retreat, or coaching session. No one gave you a framework for reading the energy of a room. No one trained your body to know when silence was more honest than speech. No one taught you how to sense the difference between a meeting that was alive and one that was merely occupied.

You know when a decision is right and still wrong. The analysis supports it. The stakeholders have been consulted. The logic is sound. And yet something in you hesitates, not because you have contrary evidence, but because the decision, for all its correctness, does not feel coherent with who the organization is trying to become. You have overridden that feeling and watched the decision corrode something you could not name. You have honored that feeling and struggled to explain why to people who wanted data.

You know when someone is telling you the truth and when they are telling you what they think you need to hear. Not from the words. From something underneath the words, a quality of attention, a steadiness in the eyes, a willingness to hold the pause after speaking that signals the speaker is not performing but present. You have sat across from people and known, in your body, that the conversation was real, and you have sat across from people and known, equally in your body, that it was not. No one taught you how to tell the difference.

And yet you know these things. Not conceptually. Experientially. You have lived inside them so many times that they feel ordinary. You have never thought of them as capacities because no one has ever called them that.

But they are.

·   ·   ·

The first thing to notice is that you recognized all of this before any word appeared for it.

Your body knew. Often it knew before language did. It knew when the room changed. It knew when the silence needed holding. It knew when you were performing instead of being present. It knew when the timing was right. The knowing was not intellectual. It was somatic, located in the chest, the gut, the shift in your breathing, the tightness or release in your shoulders. The knowing came first. Language, if it came at all, arrived later, inadequate, approximate, slightly wrong.

This is important. Because the capacities that matter most in leadership are the ones that resist language.

Try to describe what happens when you walk into a room and it changes. Try to explain, in precise terms, what you are sensing when you know the meeting is alive. Try to put into words what your body is telling you when it says hold the silence. The words are never quite right. They either reduce the experience to something smaller than what it is, "presence," "charisma," "emotional intelligence," or they abstract it into something larger, "leadership style," "influence," "soft skills." Either way, the lived experience escapes the container.

This is not a failure of language. It is a feature of the capacities themselves.

They resist naming because they were not built through naming. They were built through contact, through years of standing in rooms and sensing what was needed, through accumulated experience that trained the nervous system to read situations the conscious mind could not yet parse. The knowing preceded the language because the knowing was formed beneath language, in the body, in the patterns of attention that developed over thousands of encounters.

Leadership scholarship tried to name these capacities anyway. It called them "emotional intelligence." It called them "executive presence." It called them "situational awareness." Each label captured something. None of them captured the thing itself.

Because the thing itself is not a trait you possess. It is a capacity you exercise, a way of being in a room that cannot be reduced to a skill, a behavior, or a competency score.

The labels arrived too early and closed what should have remained experiential. They turned a living capacity into a static attribute and then tried to measure it, which is like trying to weigh a conversation or time a feeling.

So let us try something different. Let us not name too quickly. Let us instead stay with what you already recognize and let the words arrive late, provisional, incomplete, slightly unsatisfying, the way they actually arrive in experience.

•   •   •

What the Body Already Knows

Start with the simplest version.

There are moments in leadership when your body knows before your mind does.

You walk into a room and your chest tightens. The meeting has not started. No one has said anything alarming. But something in your body has already registered that the room is not right. Maybe it is the angle of someone's shoulders. Maybe it is the quality of the quiet, not relaxed but held. Maybe it is something you could never identify even if you tried. Your body read the room before you consciously entered it.

This is not intuition in the vague sense. This is the nervous system doing what it was trained to do, reading micro-signals, processing patterns beneath conscious awareness, and producing a felt sense that arrives as sensation rather than thought. Tightness. Openness. Weight. Lightness. The body registers yes or the body registers not-yet. The shoulders say this is safe or the shoulders say be careful.

Most leaders have been trained to override this. To privilege data over sensation, analysis over felt sense, the brain over the body. And so the capacity atrophies, not because it disappears, but because it is ignored so consistently that it stops being trusted. The body still knows. The leader just stops listening.

But sometimes, in the moments that matter most, the body insists. The merger is announced, and three hundred people are looking at you, and your body tells you, before any plan forms, what the room needs. Not information. Not reassurance. Something else. Something that lives in how you stand, how you breathe, how you meet their eyes. Your body knows that this moment requires a quality of presence that cannot be faked, and either you have that quality available or you do not. It was either formed in you through years of practice, or it was not.

Here is the first recognition: the body is not a vehicle for the mind. It is an instrument of perception.

And like any instrument, it can be trained, tuned, to perceive more, to hold more, to respond with greater precision and coherence. Or it can be neglected, in which case it still perceives, still holds, still responds, but roughly, reactively, without the refinement that practice would have produced.

Artists know this. They train the body as a perceptual instrument before they train it as an expressive one. The dancer learns to feel the floor before learning to leave it. The singer learns to feel the breath before learning to shape it.

Leaders are almost never trained this way. And yet every leader relies on this instrument in every critical moment. They rely on a body they have never deliberately trained to do the work it is already doing.

•　　•　　•

Different Moments Ask for Different Things

Now notice something else you already know: the quality of what is needed changes depending on the moment.

The room after the layoff announcement does not ask for the same thing as the room where the team is stalling. The one-on-

one with the person you are losing does not ask for what the board meeting asks for. The moment of crisis does not ask for what the moment of celebration asks for. You have felt these differences. You have adjusted for them, sometimes skillfully, sometimes not.

In one moment, what is needed is to stay. To remain present when everything in you wants to retreat, to armor, to manage, to control.

You have been in this room. The announcement has just been made, the restructuring, the loss, the decision that cannot be reversed. Three hundred people are looking at you. Some are angry. Some are afraid. Some have gone blank in the way people go blank when the body absorbs a blow the mind has not yet processed. And you are standing in front of them, and what they need from you is not a plan. Not yet. What they need is for you to be here. Actually here. Not performing steadiness but standing inside the same difficulty they are standing inside, without collapsing under it, without retreating behind your role, without rushing to the reassurance that would make you feel better but would make them feel managed.

Your body wants to leave. Not the room, the moment. The chest tightens. The shoulders lift toward the ears. Something in you begins composing the next sentence, the transition, the pivot to action, anything to escape the weight of standing in the silence with three hundred people who are afraid. But staying means not doing any of that. It means breathing. Feeling the floor under your feet. Letting the silence hold what needs holding. Meeting their eyes without flinching.

And if you can stay, if whatever has been formed in you is sufficient to hold this, something happens in the room. The fear does not disappear. But it changes shape. It becomes shared rather than isolated. People begin to breathe. Someone's shoulders drop. The silence, which felt unbearable ten seconds ago, begins to feel like ground. You have not said anything. You have not fixed anything. But the room is different because you stayed. And staying was not a technique. It was a capacity, one that was either built in you through years of practice or was not available when the moment demanded it.

Notice: in that same room, you are not only staying. You are also reading, sensing the anger in the front row, the numbness in the back, the person on the left who is about to cry. You are sensing the room's rhythm, when the silence has done its work and the next beat is approaching, the moment when speech will serve rather than intrude. And when you do speak, what comes out is not information but meaning, a frame that makes the loss survivable, a story that acknowledges what has happened without pretending it is anything other than what it is. Presence and attunement and timing and meaning, operating simultaneously, inseparable in the moment.

Other moments ask for different qualities in the foreground. There are moments when what is primary is not staying but sensing, when the team reports alignment but your body feels something else, a flatness, a held quality in the room that tells you the agreement is hollow. There are moments when what is primary is acting before the situation resolves, moving forward without a map because the map is not coming, and the felt coherence in your body is the only guide available. There are moments when meaning is primary, when facts are insufficient, and people need not information but a frame that makes the information livable. There are moments when restraint is primary, when the hardest thing, harder than action or speech, is to wait, holding the tension without resolving it, trusting that what needs to emerge will emerge if given time.

You know these moments are not the same. You adjust for them constantly, modulating your voice, your posture, your pace, the quality of your attention. You do this without being taught because your body has learned, through years of leading, that different pressures require different capacities. You cannot stay the same person in every room. The work asks you to change, not who you are, but how you are available. And the range of that availability, the breadth of what you can offer, depends on what has been formed in you.

And in the moments you remember most, the ones that changed something in you or in the people around you, what was needed was all of these at once. Presence and attunement and timing and meaning and restraint, woven together so seamlessly that separating them would be like trying to separate the colors in white light. In those moments, you were not exercising individual skills. You were operating from a coherence that held multiple capacities simultaneously, a coherence that felt, when it was available, effortless, and that felt, when it was not, impossible to manufacture.

•   •   •

Why These Could Not Be Taught

You may have noticed something about the capacities described above: they do not yield to instruction.

You cannot teach someone to stay present by explaining what presence is. You can explain it perfectly, the neuroscience of it, the somatic markers, the difference between performed composure and actual grounded attention, and the person will nod and understand and still be unable to do it when the room goes tense. Because the capacity is not located in understanding. It is located in the nervous system's trained response to pressure. And that trained response cannot be installed through explanation. It can only be formed through repeated exposure to the conditions that demand it.

You cannot teach someone to sense what a room is holding. You can give them frameworks for emotional intelligence, active listening techniques, empathy models, and they will apply them diligently and still miss the thing that matters. Because what the room is holding is not legible to a framework. It is legible to a body that has been trained to feel it, a body that has stood in enough rooms, under enough pressure, with enough at stake, that its perceptual range has expanded beyond what any framework could capture.

You cannot teach someone to act before certainty arrives. You can train decision-making processes, risk analysis, scenario planning, rapid prototyping, and they will be useful. But they will not produce the capacity to move forward when the analysis is incomplete and the only available guide is a felt coherence that lives beneath articulation. That capacity is formed through the accumulated experience of acting under uncertainty and discovering, again and again, that the body's coherence was reliable even when the mind's certainty was not.

You cannot teach someone to offer meaning. You can teach communication skills, framing, storytelling, message architecture, and they will produce competent communication. But competent communication and meaning are not the same thing. Meaning arrives when the person speaking has felt what the room needs to feel and has found a way to give it form, not just verbal form but embodied form, the form that comes from standing inside the truth of the situation rather than narrating it from outside.

This is why leadership development has been so frustrating. Not because it teaches the wrong things. Because the things that matter most cannot be taught at all, not through instruction, not through frameworks, not through workshops or coaching or 360-degree feedback. They can only be formed. Built slowly, through sustained contact with practices that demand the practitioner change, not their knowledge, but themselves.

You have probably experienced this frustration directly. You attended the workshop on executive presence and understood everything that was said. You left with tools and frameworks and an action plan. And the next time you walked into a room where presence was required, where three hundred people needed something from you that no tool could provide, the workshop was not available. What was available was whatever had been formed in you before the workshop. The understanding was in your mind. The capacity was either in your body or it was not.

And when it was not, the gap was not neutral. It cost something.

It cost the room its ground. It cost the team the truth it needed to hear, delivered in a way it could receive. It cost the leader another layer of distance between who they were performing and who they actually were.

The absence of formation does not leave a blank space. It leaves a wound that looks, from the outside, like competence.

And this is what the previous chapter established: a lineage of practices already exists that does build these capacities, not through explanation but through formation. It has been forming human beings for these exact conditions, presence under exposure, judgment before certainty, meaning without proof, coherence when the ground shifts, for centuries.

The question is not whether these capacities can be developed. They can. They are developed every day, in rehearsal rooms, in studios, in practice spaces where human beings are formed for the constraint that will not relent.

The question is whether leadership will claim this lineage.

•   •   •

Words are beginning to arrive. Let them come slowly.

There is something that might be called presence, the capacity to remain in the body, in the room, in the moment, without retreating into performance or self-protection. You recognized it earlier when you described the difference between performing leadership and actually leading.

It is not a trait. It is not confidence. It is a trained availability.

A nervous system that has learned to stay when pressure says leave.

There is something that might be called attunement, the capacity to sense what is happening in the space between people, beneath what is being said, beyond what is being shown. You recognized it when you described feeling the room's unspoken truth, sensing that the agreement was hollow, reading the posture and breath and eyes of the person you were losing.

It is not empathy exactly. It is closer to perception.

A sensitivity to the relational field that has been refined through practice until it operates faster than thought.

There is something that might be called judgment, not the decision-making kind, not the analytical weighing of options, but the aesthetic kind. The capacity to sense what a moment needs before the moment has declared itself. To know that this word, this pause, this gesture will land, and that one will not. You recognized it when you described timing, when you felt the difference between the feedback that landed on Thursday and the feedback that would have failed on Monday. It is the capacity to discern coherence, to sense what belongs and what does not, what will serve and what will fragment.

There is something that might be called rhythm, a relationship to time that is felt rather than measured. The capacity to sense when to move and when to stay, when to compress and when to expand, when silence is the most honest response, and when it becomes avoidance. You recognized it every time you described a moment where timing mattered more than content.

There is something that might be called meaning-making, the capacity to offer not just information but a frame that makes the information livable. To sense what people need to feel in order to act, and to give that feeling a shape it can hold. You recognized it when you described the moments that changed something, when leadership became not just direction but orientation, not just communication but communion.

There may be more. There almost certainly are. Something about the weight of consequence, the capacity to feel the ethical gravity of a decision before it is made. Something about the willingness to stay inside difficulty when every instinct says resolve it. Something about what it means to carry an organization's meaning in your body, not as a message you deliver but as a coherence you embody.

These words are arriving late and arriving incomplete. They do not yet form a system. They do not yet make a framework. They are provisional labels for experiences you have already lived, and each one feels slightly smaller than the experience it is trying to name.

That is how it should feel. Because these capacities were not built to be named. They were built to be exercised. And the distance between the name and the thing named is the distance between knowing about leadership and actually leading.

•   •   •

There is one more thing to notice.

You have been recognizing these capacities as though they were always yours, personal qualities, individual traits, things you happen to have or happen to lack. But they are not personal. They are not individual. They are human capacities that appear wherever the constraint appears, wherever people must hold judgment, meaning, and presence under conditions that cannot be resolved by rules, speed, or certainty.

They appear in artists who have trained for decades. They appear in leaders who have led through enough crises to be changed by them. They appear in teachers, nurses, chaplains, and anyone whose work demands that they meet another human being in difficulty and offer something that no procedure can specify. They appear wherever the work demands formation, not just instruction.

And they are not added to a person in the moment. They are revealed under load.

The load does not create them. It exposes what has been formed and what has not. What was built slowly, through sustained contact with a demanding practice. And what was left unbuilt, which shows up as the gap, the hollowness, the composure that has no ground beneath it.

These capacities are not added to a leader.

They are revealed by what the work demands.

And they are waiting.

SIX

What It Costs to Hold

The weight of capacity under pressure

There is a version of leadership that no one talks about.

Not the version where you make the hard call and it turns out to be right. Not the version where you stand before the room and the room responds. Not the version where your presence holds, your timing lands, the words come, and they are true.

The other version. The one where you are standing in the same room, facing the same people, carrying the same weight, and it is not working.

You are present. You are trying to be present. But something in your body is clenched, and it will not release. The room can feel it. You can feel them feeling it. There is a distance opening between you and the people you are supposed to be holding, and the distance is not strategic or intentional; it is the gap between what the moment requires and what you have available to offer. You are reaching for a capacity that is not there. Not because you never had it, but because right now, under this pressure, in this room, with this much at stake, it is not enough.

This is what capacity looks like under load.

Not elegant. Not quiet.

Not the stillness of the conductor before the downbeat. This is the conductor whose hands are shaking. This is the director who knows the second act is false and cannot find the question that will make it true. This is the storyteller who has misjudged the room and can feel the community's coherence fraying in real time.

No one writes about this version. The leadership literature describes the moments when capacity is present. The artistry literature describes the moments when formation has done its work. But the moments that matter most, the moments that reveal what formation actually costs, are the moments when it is not enough. When the practitioner reaches for what was supposed to be there and the reaching comes up short.

This chapter lives inside those moments.

Consider what it means to hold.

Not to act. Not to decide. Not to solve. To hold. To stand inside a situation that has no resolution and to remain present to it without collapsing into performance, without retreating into control, without offering the premature reassurance that would relieve the pressure for you but would betray the truth of what the room is living.

You have done this. You have sat in the meeting where the news was irreversibly bad, and there was nothing to say that would make it better. You have stood in front of people who were frightened and looked to you not for answers, they knew you did not have answers, but for evidence that someone was willing to remain inside the fear with them. You have held the phone call where the person on the other end was breaking, and the only thing you could offer was the quality of your attention, your willingness to stay, to not rush, to not fix, to simply be present to what was happening.

Holding looks like nothing from the outside. It produces no visible output. There is no deliverable. No decision point. No action item. A performance review cannot capture it. A 360-degree assessment cannot measure it. And because it is invisible, it is undervalued, treated as the absence of action rather than what it actually is: one of the most demanding capacities in human work.

Because holding is not passive. Holding is the sustained act of remaining present while every instinct says move, fix, speak, resolve. It requires a nervous system that has been trained to sustain the weight of unresolved difficulty, trained through practice, through repeated exposure to conditions where resolution was not available, and the only option was to stay.

And the weight accumulates. This is the part that no one talks about. Each moment of holding does not end when the meeting ends or the call is over or you walk to your car. It leaves a trace in the body.

The weight of having held three hundred people's fear. The weight of having sat with someone's grief without offering relief.

The weight of having known the truth and not been able to speak it because the room was not ready.

These weights do not dissolve. They accumulate. And the leader carries them, in their shoulders, in their jaw, in the quality of their sleep, in the slow narrowing of their emotional range, because there is no place to set them down.

No one in the organization is positioned to hold what the leader holds. That is what makes it leadership. And that is what makes it costly.

Leaders do not speak about this cost. Not because they are stoic. Because there is no language for it. The vocabulary of leadership has words for strategy, execution, alignment, engagement. It does not have words for what it feels like to hold an organization's anxiety in your body for months at a time. For the specific exhaustion that comes not from doing too much but from carrying too much. For the loneliness of being watched while not knowing, of being the person everyone looks to for certainty when certainty is not available, and feeling the weight of their looking.

And when holding fails, when the weight exceeds what was formed, the failure is not dramatic. It is quiet. A slight tightening in the voice. A sentence offered half a beat too early. A reassurance that sounds right but feels hollow. The room registers the failure before the leader does. Something in the collective attention shifts, a subtle withdrawal, a recalibration of trust. The people in the room adjust their expectations downward. Not because the leader said the wrong thing. Because the leader's body could not hold what the moment was asking it to hold.

When Capacity Is Misread

The capacities described in the previous chapter, presence, attunement, judgment, rhythm, meaning-making, carry a cost that is rarely acknowledged: they are routinely mistaken for something else.

Presence is mistaken for passivity. The leader who remains still when the room wants action, who holds silence when the culture expects decisiveness, who stands inside difficulty rather than rushing to resolve it: this leader is not seen as present. They are seen as frozen. As weak. As failing to lead. The feedback arrives in familiar language: "We need more urgency." "The team needs direction." "You seemed hesitant in there." What the feedback cannot see is that the stillness was not hesitation. It was the hardest thing the leader did that day.

Attunement is mistaken for indecision. The leader who senses that the room's agreement is hollow, who feels the misalignment beneath the words, and slows down rather than driving forward. Who asks the question no one wants asked. This leader is not seen as attuned. They are seen as inefficient. The culture rewards execution. The culture punishes the leader who senses that execution without alignment will produce compliance without commitment.

Restraint is mistaken for lack of confidence. The leader who does not answer immediately. Who sits with the question. Who says "I don't know yet" when the room wants certainty. This leader is not seen as someone who has the capacity to hold ambiguity. They are seen as someone who does not have the answer. The distinction is invisible to a culture that equates speed with strength and certainty with competence.

And meaning-making is mistaken for sentimentality. The leader who speaks about what the loss means, not the business impact, not the strategic implications, but what it means for the people in the room, is not seen as someone offering something essential. They are seen as soft. Because in most organizational cultures, what matters is what can be measured. And meaning cannot be measured. It can only be felt.

This mismatch is not incidental. It is structural.

The capacities that formation builds are precisely the capacities that performance cultures cannot recognize. And because they cannot be recognized, they cannot be valued. And because they cannot be valued, the leaders who exercise them pay a reputational cost for doing the thing the moment actually required.

You have lived this. You have been the leader who slowed down when the culture wanted speed, who asked the uncomfortable question, who held the meeting open past its scheduled end because something real was emerging. And afterward, in the hallway, the feedback: "That felt unproductive." "We need to be more efficient." "What was the outcome?" The outcome was that for six minutes, the team was actually in the room together. Actually listening. Actually willing to say what they had been holding. But that outcome has no metric. It appears on no dashboard. And the leader who created the conditions for it is evaluated as though they wasted time.

Over years, this penalty reshapes the leader. Not through a single correction but through the slow accretion of signals: don't do that. Move faster. Produce outcomes. Show decisiveness. And the leader's range narrows. The capacities are still there; they can still feel the room, still sense the timing, still know when the silence needs holding. But the cost of exercising those capacities becomes too high. The leader learns to perform the version of leadership that the culture rewards. And the version the culture rewards is the version that does not require formation. That requires only performance.

This is part of what makes formation costly. Not just the internal weight of holding. But the external penalty for holding in a world that rewards performing.

•   •   •

The Cost of Getting It Wrong

Now something harder.

The capacities the previous chapter named are not virtues. They are not reliably good. They are not guarantees. They are capacities, which means they can be exercised well or badly, and the difference is not always visible from the inside.

Presence can arrive too late; the room has already made its judgment by the time you arrive as yourself. Silence can be held too long, past the point where it serves and into the territory where it frightens. Attunement can misfire, what you named as the room's truth was your own projection, and the room felt exposed rather than seen. Timing can be wrong by half a beat, and the near-miss of timing is sometimes worse than a clear failure because the room senses the effort and the failure simultaneously.

But the misfire that costs the most is the one that feels, in the moment, like the right thing to do.

Meaning offered prematurely.

You are standing in the room after the announcement. The restructuring. The loss. Whatever it is, it is done. The people in the room are in it. Some are crying quietly. Some are staring at nothing. Some are already withdrawing into self-preservation because the alternative, staying present to what is happening, is unbearable.

And you feel, in your body, the impulse to help. Not the strategic impulse. The human one. The one that says: these people are in pain, and I can offer something that will make the pain mean something. I can frame this. I can tell them that this is hard, but we will come through it. The relief of saying it, of moving from standing-inside-the-pain to making-sense-of-the-pain, is almost physical. Your chest wants to open. Your voice wants to offer.

So you offer. You speak the meaning. You frame the loss. Your voice is steady. The words are right. And the moment you finish, you feel it: a slight withdrawal in the room. Not resistance. Something quieter. A closing. The people are still looking at you. But something behind their eyes has shifted. They are performing reception of what you said.

What happened is precise: the room was still inside the pain. The pain had not yet been fully felt. It was still arriving, still being absorbed, still finding its shape in each person's body. And you interrupted that process. Not with something false. With something true. But truth offered before the body is ready to receive it does not land as meaning. It lands as management.

The meaning you offered, however beautiful, became the thing that separated you from the people you were trying to hold. You reached for meaning because meaning was less costly than presence. And the room knew.

These are not catastrophic failures. They are the ordinary misfires of capacity under pressure. And they matter because they disabuse us of the fantasy that formation produces mastery. It does not. Formation produces capacity, and capacity, under sufficient pressure, can still fail. The conductor's hands still shake. The director still misjudges the scene. The storyteller still loses the room. The difference is not that formation eliminates failure. The difference is that formation allows the practitioner to return after failure, to feel the misfire, absorb its cost, and come back to the work changed by what they got wrong.

But here is what no one says about these failures: they do not get easier. The leader who has been formed enough to recognize that their presence arrived too late does not feel less pain about it. They feel more. Because formation increases sensitivity. The more attuned you become, the more precisely you can feel your own misfires. The more present you become, the more fully you inhabit your own failures.

Formation does not shield you from the cost of getting it wrong. It makes the cost more precise, more inescapable, more felt.

This is the reckoning that capacity demands: the better you become at holding, the more you know about the moments when you could not hold. The more you can sense what a room needs, the more you are aware of the rooms where you could not provide it. The cost of growing is knowing more clearly what growth has not yet reached.

•　　•　　•

And then there are the moments when the holding works.

The silence lands. The room shifts. You feel the collective breathing change. The person who was about to leave the conversation stays. The team, which entered the meeting defended and separate, begins to soften into something more honest. You did not do anything dramatic. You stayed. You held. You let the silence do its work. And when you finally spoke, the words came from a place that was not performing, a place that was simply present to what the room was living. The words landed. Not perfectly. But truly. The room received them. Something moved that had been stuck.

No one applauds. No one says, "That was a great moment of leadership." The meeting ends. People stand up. They gather their things. Some nod at you. Some do not. The moment is already dissolving into the next task, the next meeting, the next demand.

And you drive home.

And you carry it. Not the satisfaction of having done it well, though there may be some of that, quiet and brief. You carry the residue of what passed through you. The room's fear. The team's grief. The unspoken thing that finally surfaced and that you held without flinching, it is still in your body. In your chest. In the heaviness behind your eyes.

You held it for them, and holding it for them meant it also passed through you.

You did not deflect it. You did not manage it. You stood inside it and let it do its work on the room, which means it also did its work on you.

You eat dinner. You are present but not entirely. Your partner asks about your day and you say fine. Not because you are hiding something. Because there is no language for what happened. No way to describe the specific weight of having held thirty people's unspoken fear in your body for forty-five minutes and let it change the room. No way to explain that the meeting worked, that something real happened, and that the cost of it working is sitting on your shoulders and will be there tomorrow.

This is what the book has been building toward. Not the cost of failure. The cost of the work itself. The cost of being the person through whom difficult truth passes on its way to being held. Formation does not eliminate this cost. Formation makes you capable of carrying it without distortion, without the weight warping your judgment, corroding your presence, narrowing your range. But the weight is real. It accumulates. And there is no version of this work where it does not.

•   •   •

Why Capacity Cannot Be Performed

There is a temptation, after recognizing these capacities, to imitate them.

To learn what presence looks like and perform it. To study what attunement sounds like and replicate it. To observe how a leader with capacity holds silence and then hold silence yourself, not because your body knows this is the moment for silence, but because you watched someone else do it and it seemed to work.

The imitation will fail. It will fail because the people in the room can feel the difference.

They cannot always name the difference. They may not be able to articulate why this leader's silence feels like holding, and that leader's silence feels like absence. Why this leader's presence feels grounding, and that leader's presence feels like a performance of calm. Why this leader's question opens the room, and that leader's identical question closes it. But their bodies know. Their trust adjusts accordingly.

The difference is not technique. The difference is ground.

When a leader has been formed, when presence has been built through years of practice under pressure, there is something beneath the visible behavior that the room can feel. A steadiness that is not performed but structural. A coherence between what the leader is showing and what they are experiencing. The room feels the absence of the gap. It registers as trustworthiness.

When a leader is performing at capacity without having been formed for it, the gap is present. The silence looks right but feels hollow. The presence looks calm, but the body is braced. The question sounds empathic, but the listening is strategic rather than genuine. And the room feels the gap, not as a conscious judgment but as a somatic registration. Something in their bodies tightens slightly. Something in their trust recalibrates.

This is why leadership development workshops produce understanding without capacity. The participants learn what to do. They can describe it, model it, and practice it in role-plays. But when the pressure arrives, when the room is charged, when the stakes are real, the learning is not available. What is available is formation. And if formation is not there, what replaces it is performance. And performance, under pressure, fractures trust.

This is not a criticism of leaders who perform. Almost everyone performs. Performance is the natural response to demands that exceed capacity. The leader who performs calm is not dishonest; they are doing their best with what they have. But doing their best with what they have is not the same as having what the moment requires. And the distance between these two is the formation gap. It is the gap this entire book is about.

You have been in rooms where you could feel the gap. Not in the leader's words, the words were fine. In their body. Something was held rather than grounded. Something was managed rather than present. The leader was working very hard to appear as though they were not working at all, and that labor was visible to every nervous system in the room, even if no mind could name it. The room did not relax. The room performed relaxation back. And the meeting ended with everyone having played their part and no one having been changed.

You have also been in rooms where the gap was absent. Where the leader's visible behavior and their interior state were aligned. In those rooms, something different happened. People told the truth. Silence was inhabited. The hard thing was said, and the room held it without shattering. Not because the leader was charismatic or inspirational or wise. Because the leader was present. Actually present. And the room's nervous system calibrated to that presence the way an orchestra calibrates to a conductor who is listening.

The difference between these two rooms is not a difference of technique. It is a difference of formation. And it cannot be bridged by learning. Only by being changed.

Most organizations have never been in the second room. They do not know what it feels like. They have spent so long inside performed leadership that performance has become the baseline, the expected texture of authority. The leader performs confidence. The team performs engagement. The meeting performs productivity. And everyone goes home carrying the residue of having spent another day inside a performance that no one acknowledged as a performance. The exhaustion this produces is real but nameless. It is the exhaustion of sustained inauthenticity, not because anyone is lying, but because the formation that would allow authenticity under pressure was never built.

•　　•　　•

There is something that changes in you when you stop thinking of leadership as something you do.

Not a sudden change. A slow one. A gradual reorientation that begins not with insight but with accumulated weight. The weight of rooms you could not hold. The weight of silences you misjudged. The weight of meaning you offered too early. The accumulation of every moment where what was required exceeded what was formed.

At some point, you may not be able to identify when leadership stops being a role and becomes a condition. Something you carry rather than something you perform. The meetings do not stop. The decisions do not stop. The people who need you to be certain when you are not certain do not stop needing that. But something in your relationship to all of it shifts. You stop pretending it is manageable. You stop performing adequacy. You begin to reckon with the actual scale of what the work asks a human being to hold.

The change is not that you become better. It is that you become honest about what it costs. Honest that presence is not a skill but a physical discipline, one that requires sustained practice to maintain and that deteriorates under neglect. Honest that attunement is not a personality trait but a perceptual capacity that can be sharp or dull depending on what has been trained.

Honest that meaning-making is not a communication strategy but an act of moral imagination that demands you feel what the room is feeling before you presume to name it. Honest that timing is not instinct but rhythm, a relationship to time that was either formed in you or was not.

Honest that these capacities cannot be assembled from components. That they are not additive. They are integrative. They operate as a whole or they fracture under pressure. And the integration is not something you achieve. It is something you undergo. Through practice. Through exposure. Through the slow, costly formation work of being changed by what you are asked to hold.

Leaders do not often speak about this weight. There is no category for it in the language of leadership. No competency framework includes "willingness to be changed by the role." No assessment measures the toll of carrying what the organization cannot carry for itself.

This is where the book is now.

Not at the beginning of understanding. The understanding arrived chapters ago. Not at the recognition of capacity. That recognition is complete. Not at the discovery of a lineage that could form these capacities. That lineage has been revealed.

The book is at the place where honesty begins.

Where the reader stops asking what these capacities are and starts reckoning with what they cost. Where the distance between knowing about leadership and actually leading becomes not an intellectual distinction but a felt weight.

Where the question is no longer "How do I develop these?" but something quieter, more honest, and harder to answer:

Am I willing to be changed by what the work requires?

It is the only question that matters now.

SEVEN

The
Ongoing Condition

What continues after the reckoning

Monday arrives.

The calendar is full. The inbox has not slowed. The meeting at nine is the same meeting it was last week, the same room, the same people, the same agenda items carried forward from the quarter before. The direct report who has been disengaging is still disengaging. The initiative that stalled in October is still stalled. The board wants the numbers by Thursday. The team wants direction by end of day.

Nothing in the world has changed.

The organizational culture that misreads presence as passivity has not reformed itself overnight. The performance review system that cannot measure what matters has not been replaced. The meetings still run to the clock rather than to the room's need. The people who want certainty from you still want certainty, and the ground beneath the certainty is still shifting.

The previous chapters asked what this work costs. What it builds. What it demands of the person who carries it.

You knew this. You did not expect the world to rearrange itself around what you now understand. Understanding has never rearranged the world. But there is a particular quality to the morning after a reckoning, a dissonance between what you now see and what the world still asks you to perform. You walk into the same building, sit at the same desk, and open the same laptop. And the distance between what you carry and what the environment can hold is wider than it was before you started reading. Before you recognized the capacities. Before you felt the cost.

This is not a failure of the reckoning. It is its consequence.

Something similar happens to anyone who has been genuinely changed by an encounter with truth. The soldier who returns from war and sits at the family dinner table. The doctor who has just lost a patient and drives to pick up groceries. The world does not adjust itself to the interior change. The world continues. And the person who has been changed must learn to carry the change inside a container that has no room for it.

This is what Monday morning feels like after a reckoning with what leadership actually costs. The container has not changed. The change is all inside. And finding a way to carry what has changed inside a world that has not is itself a form of practice, one that no workshop will ever teach, because it can only be learned by living it.

You cannot unknow what you now know. You cannot unfeel what the last chapters asked you to feel. The recognition of capacity, the pressure of holding, the cost of getting it wrong, the impossibility of performance bridging the distance to formation, these are not ideas you can set aside when the calendar fills. They are alterations in perception. And altered perception does not negotiate with schedules.

The nine o'clock meeting will proceed as scheduled. The people around the table will speak in the language the culture provides, alignment, deliverables, action items, and next steps. And you will participate. You will use the same language. You will nod at the appropriate moments and offer the expected inputs. But underneath the participation, something will be different. You will feel the room in a way you cannot turn off. You will sense the distance between what is being said and what is being lived. You will notice the moment when someone performs agreement and you will know, in your body, not your mind, that the agreement is hollow. And you will face the quiet choice that will recur every day from now on: do you name what you see, or do you let the meeting proceed?

Most of the time, you will let the meeting proceed. Not because you are cowardly. Because naming what you see would require something from the room that the room is not yet ready to provide. Because the distance between your altered perception and the culture's operating assumptions is wider than any single meeting can bridge. Because formation does not give you the right to disrupt. It gives you the capacity to see, and seeing, without the ability to act on what you see, is its own kind of load.

So here you are. On Monday. In the same world. Carrying something different.

•　　•　　•

What Is Subtly Different Now

You enter the room and you notice what you enter.

Not strategically. Not because you are applying a framework. Because something in your attention has shifted and the shift cannot be reversed. You feel the room's temperature before anyone speaks. You register the quality of the silence, whether it is relaxed or held, whether people are present or already elsewhere. You notice posture. Not as body language to be decoded but as information arriving in your own body, a tightness in your chest that tells you the room is braced, a softening in your shoulders that tells you the room is open.

You noticed some of this before. But you notice it differently now. Before, it was background noise, sensory data that arrived without a category, that you registered and then overrode in favor of the agenda. Now it is foreground. Not because you are trying to make it foreground. Because the work of formation has stripped away one layer of the override. The body's signals are slightly louder. The mind's dismissal of them is slightly less automatic.

This is not mastery. This is not even competence. It is a slight recalibration of attention. A fraction of a degree. And yet the fraction matters, because a fraction of a degree in attention is the difference between hearing what the room is saying and hearing only what is being said.

You listen differently.

Not better, necessarily. But with a different quality of patience. Where you once listened for content, for the information embedded in what people were saying, you now also listen for what is underneath the content. The hesitation before the sentence. The words that were chosen and the words that were avoided. The energy in the room that does not match the words being spoken. You cannot always read it accurately. You misread it often. But you are listening for it, and listening for it is not the same as not listening for it.

You resist differently.

The impulse to fix is still there. The impulse to speak, to reassure, to offer meaning, to move the meeting toward resolution, these impulses have not disappeared. They fire with the same urgency they always have. But now there is a space between the impulse and the action. A small space. Half a second, maybe less. Where the impulse fires and you feel it fire and you do not immediately obey it. Where you sense the pull toward premature meaning and you recognize it, not always in time, not always successfully, but you recognize it as premature rather than experiencing it as natural. The space is not control. It is awareness. And awareness, even when it does not change the outcome, changes the quality of the engagement.

You hold silence differently.

Not longer, necessarily. Not more skillfully. But with a different relationship to what the silence contains. Where silence once felt like absence, like dead air to be filled, it now sometimes feels like substance. Like the room is doing something in the silence that it cannot do while someone is speaking. You do not always trust this feeling. You still fill silences that should have been held. You still break the quiet when the quiet was doing its work. But you are aware that the silence had work to do. And that awareness, however imperfect, is new.

None of these shifts are dramatic. None of them would be visible in a performance review. No one in the room would say, "Something is different about you." The shifts are internal, micro-adjustments in attention, patience, resistance, and continuity that alter the texture of your presence without producing any measurable outcome.

And yet the texture matters. The people in the room may not be able to name what has changed, but their bodies register it. Something in your attention is slightly more available. Something in your silence is slightly less defensive. Something in your questions has shifted from interrogation to genuine inquiry, not always, not reliably, but often enough that the room's relationship to you is beginning to recalibrate. Not through any dramatic intervention. Through the accumulated effect of a presence that is marginally more honest than it was.

This is what formation looks like from the inside: not transformation but recalibration. The same leader in the same room doing what appears to be the same work, but doing it from a slightly different place. A place where the body's signals are attended to rather than overridden. Where the impulse to perform is recognized rather than obeyed. Where the silence is inhabited rather than endured. The changes are so gradual that they could be attributed to experience, to maturity, to the natural evolution of any long career. And perhaps that is what they are. Perhaps formation is simply the name for what happens when a human being submits to the demands of their work long enough to be changed by them.

•　　•　　•

The Loneliness That Remains

You are still alone in this.

That has not changed. The loneliness of authority, of being the person who holds what the organization cannot hold for itself, is not relieved by understanding what it is. Understanding does not provide company. It provides clarity, which is a different thing and sometimes a harder one. Before, the loneliness was vague, a diffuse sense of isolation that you attributed to the role, to the demands, to the nature of leadership. Now the loneliness is specific. You can name what you are carrying. You can feel its contour with precision. And precision does not lighten the load.

But something about the loneliness has changed shape.

Before, the loneliness felt like a symptom, evidence that something was wrong, that you were doing it incorrectly, that a better leader would not feel this isolated. You compared yourself to leaders who seemed confident, connected, unburdened. You assumed they had solved something you had not. You interpreted your loneliness as personal failure.

Now you know it is structural.

The loneliness is not a symptom of poor leadership. It is a condition of the work itself. It is what happens when you are the person through whom the organization's unspoken difficulty must pass. When you are the one who holds the fear the team cannot yet face, the ambiguity the board cannot yet tolerate, the truth the culture cannot yet absorb. Someone must hold these things. And the person who holds them is, by definition, alone with them, because holding them means carrying what others have not yet been able to carry.

This does not make the loneliness easier. But it makes it legible. You stop interpreting it as failure and begin recognizing it as inherent. You stop looking for the version of leadership that eliminates loneliness and begin reckoning with the version that carries it deliberately. The loneliness becomes not something to escape but a signal to attend to, a measure of the pressure you are carrying and the question of whether your formation is sufficient to carry it without distortion.

There is a difference between lonely and alone. Lonely is the isolation that comes from believing no one understands. Alone is the solitude that comes from understanding what you are holding. Leaders who have not reckoned with the cost of this work are lonely. Leaders who have reckoned with it are alone. The distinction is not comfort. It is clarity.

And clarity, for all its coldness, has one virtue: it does not corrode. Loneliness, the unnamed, unacknowledged, vaguely shaming kind, corrodes everything it touches. It narrows the leader's range. It erodes their capacity for attunement. It makes them brittle where they need to be flexible and defended where they need to be open. The loneliness that has been reckoned with, that has been named, felt, and carried deliberately, does not corrode in the same way. It is heavy. It is real. But it is honest. And honesty, unlike denial, does not erode the capacity it asks you to carry.

There is one more thing that changes about loneliness when it becomes legible: you begin to recognize it in others. The leader across the table at the conference who pauses a beat too long before answering, you see them now. The colleague who holds the meeting open when everyone else wants to close, you understand the cost. The person who sits quietly after the presentation while everyone else networks, you know what they are carrying. Not because they told you. Because the load is recognizable to anyone who carries it. This recognition does not eliminate the solitude. But it alters it. The aloneness becomes less singular. You are alone in the room. But you are not alone in the condition.

•　　•　　•

What Can Now Be Carried

Something has expanded. Not dramatically. Not triumphantly. But measurably, if the measure is felt rather than scored.

You can sit with ambiguity longer than you could before. Not because you have become comfortable with it. Comfort is not the mechanism. But the threshold at which ambiguity triggers the compulsion to resolve has shifted slightly upward. Where you once needed to decide by Tuesday, you can now wait until Thursday, not because the answer has become clearer, but because your nervous system's capacity to remain functional without resolution has increased by a margin. The margin is small. But in the moments that matter, the margin is everything.

You can remain visible without armor for slightly longer. The scrutiny has not lessened. The exposure has not decreased. But the impulse to defend, to explain, to justify, fires with fractionally less urgency. You can feel it fire and choose, sometimes, not to respond to it. You can let the scrutiny land without immediately constructing a defense. This is not courage. It is capacity, the nervous system's trained ability to sustain exposure without collapsing into self-protection.

You can sense your own performance more quickly. Before, you could go hours, sometimes days, performing composure without recognizing that you were performing. Now the recognition arrives sooner. Not immediately. You still perform. Everyone still performs. But the distance between the performance and the awareness of the performance has narrowed. You catch yourself performing certainty and you notice the catching. The noticing does not always change the behavior. But it changes the relationship to the behavior. And changed relationship is the beginning of changed capacity.

You can let a meeting end without resolution and not experience the lack of resolution as failure. This is quieter than it sounds. For years, the unresolved meeting triggered anxiety, the sense that something should have been decided, that leadership meant driving to conclusion. Now, sometimes, not always, the unresolved meeting feels honest rather than failed. The questions were real. The room could not yet answer them. And leaving the questions open was not an abdication of leadership. It was an acknowledgment that the situation had not yet declared what it needed.

And sometimes, briefly, the work simply works. Not perfectly. Not dramatically. But the room arrives, and you arrive inside it, and something meets. The silence holds without effort. The question lands without calculation. The team, for six minutes, is actually together, actually present, actually willing. These moments do not last. They do not accumulate into mastery. But they remind you that the formation is not only cost. It is also contact, the rare, brief experience of meeting the work from a place that is sufficient. That experience, however fleeting, is what makes the return possible.

These are not achievements. They are not proof that formation is working. They are consequences, the residue of having reckoned honestly with what the work requires, of having felt the cost without turning away, of having recognized that the capacities this work demands are not added to a person but revealed by sustained contact with the conditions that require them.

The consequences are modest. They do not announce themselves. There is no moment of transformation, no breakthrough, no felt sense of "now I am different." There is only the quiet accumulation of slightly altered responses, a half-second more patience here, a fraction more capacity for exposure there, a marginally earlier recognition that the impulse to fix is firing and the situation does not yet need fixing.

But the gap is slightly different now. Not narrower, exactly. More honest.

More clearly seen. More precisely felt. And a distance that is precisely felt can be worked with. A distance that is denied or unrecognized cannot.

•　　•　　•

There is no moment when this becomes easy.

This is not a sentence the book offers as consolation or as warning. It is a description of the territory. The demands that revealed the formation gap did not create a temporary crisis. They revealed a permanent condition. The world that requires leaders to hold judgment, meaning, and presence under conditions of irreducible uncertainty is not reverting to something more manageable. The complexity is not temporary. The ambiguity is not a phase.

And so the question the previous chapter asked, am I willing to be changed by what the work requires, is not a question that is answered once. It is answered every morning. Every time the calendar fills and the inbox demands and the meeting at nine requires something from you that no preparation can guarantee. Every time the room needs holding and your capacity to hold is either there or it is not. The question is not behind you. It is the ongoing condition of the work.

Formation does not resolve this condition. It changes the quality of your presence inside it. It does not make the load lighter. It makes you more capable of carrying it without the pressure distorting who you are, without the loneliness corroding your attunement, without the exposure collapsing your presence, without the ambiguity eroding your judgment. But the demand is still there. Every morning.

Artists know this. The dancer who has trained for twenty years does not arrive at rehearsal free of the constraint. The constraint is there, the body's resistance, the choreography's demands, the exposure of the stage. What has changed is not the constraint. What has changed is the dancer's relationship to the constraint. They enter the room knowing what it will ask. They do not flinch from it. They do not pretend it is not there. They have been changed by years of sustained contact with it, and the change has made them capable of meeting it without breaking, though not without cost. Always with cost.

And still they return. Every morning. To the barre, to the studio, to the rehearsal room where the mirrors reflect what they would rather not see, and the floor is hard under the body, and the work begins again. Not because it has become pleasurable. Not because mastery has eliminated the constraint. Because the work is their formation. Because the person they are becoming through the work is the person the work requires. And the only alternative to continuing the formation is to stop, to let the capacity atrophy, to let the performance substitute for the presence, to let the distance widen between what the moment demands and what they have available to offer.

This is the condition the book has been preparing the reader for. Not mastery. Not readiness. Not even competence. But orientation. The capacity to stand inside the work with eyes open, seeing the cost, feeling the pressure, acknowledging the loneliness, and continuing anyway. Not because the work has become bearable. Because the alternative, performing leadership without formation, carrying the demand without the capacity to carry it, leading from the distance between what is required and what is available, is no longer possible once you have seen it clearly.

You cannot go back to not knowing. You cannot return to the version of leadership that did not feel the cost. The performance that used to suffice no longer suffices, not because anyone told you it was insufficient, but because you can now feel the insufficiency in your own body. The distance is visible. The load is named. The loneliness is structural.

What remains is not a program. Not a practice regimen. Not a set of exercises that will close the gap.

What remains is the willingness to return.

To walk into the room tomorrow. To feel the room's demand. To resist the impulse to perform. To stay present to what is happening, or to fail to stay present and to know you failed and to return the next day and try again. To live inside the ongoing condition of a work that asks you to be more than you have been formed to be, and to keep submitting to the formation anyway.

The willingness to return is not a virtue. It is not noble or admirable. It is simply the thing that separates leaders who continue to deepen from leaders who begin to calcify. The calcification is not dramatic. It happens quietly, a gradual narrowing, a slow substitution of performance for presence, a barely perceptible closing of the very capacities that the work once opened. It happens to good people. It happens to skilled leaders. It happens whenever the cost of remaining open exceeds the formation available to carry it, and the leader, without deciding to, without even noticing, begins to close.

The willingness to return is the refusal to close. Not a dramatic refusal. A daily one. Mundane. Repeated. Unglamorous. The choice, each morning, to enter the room again, knowing what it will cost, knowing that the capacity to meet it is imperfect, knowing that today may be the day when the holding fails, and entering anyway.

Not because it gets easier.

Because you are no longer willing to live without it.

EIGHT
Inside *the Work*

You wake carrying yesterday.

Not the facts of it. The facts are already fading. They belong to the part of the mind that moves on. What you are carrying is not information. It is residue. A weight that lives in the body, not the mind. A heaviness behind the eyes that sleep did not fully reach.

Yesterday you spoke too soon.

You know this because your body told you last night, in the car, in the minutes before sleep, in the particular quality of the silence between you and the thought you kept returning to. It was not a catastrophic error. No one noticed. The meeting continued. The conversation landed somewhere acceptable. Professional. Adequate. But you felt the moment when your words arrived before the room was ready to receive them. You felt the slight closing. The almost imperceptible adjustment in the other person's posture, a settling back, a quarter inch of withdrawal that meant the opening you had sensed was no longer there.

A year ago you would not have felt this. The meeting would have ended, and you would have moved on, filed it under "went fine," and carried nothing into the evening. You did not use to carry this. You notice what you used to miss. The micro-shifts in the room's attention. The difference between a silence that is held and a silence that is merely empty. The precise moment when your words served the room and the precise moment when they served your own need to contribute. You see these things now. And seeing them means you carry them, because what you see clearly you cannot set down easily.

This is what no one told you about growth: it does not feel like progress. It feels like additional weight. You perceive more, which means you register more, which means more of the day stays in your body after the day ends. The leader you were five years ago went home lighter. Not because the work was lighter. Because the instrument was less refined. A blunt instrument registers less. A tuned instrument registers everything. You have been tuning for years, through the rooms you held and the rooms you couldn't hold, through the silences that taught you and the failures that changed you, and the result is not ease. The result is that Wednesday morning arrives and you are already carrying something.

You shower. You dress. You move through the morning without thinking about what is ahead because you have done this enough times that the preparation is no longer conscious. The body prepares itself. The shoulders settle into the posture that will carry you through the first meeting. The jaw, which you did not notice was clenched, releases slightly when you become aware of it. The breath, which had been running shallow since you opened your eyes, deepens by a fraction when you stand at the counter and wait for the coffee.

You are not anxious. You are not dreading the day. The day is ordinary. That is precisely the point. The rooms you will enter today are not crisis rooms. They are the rooms that make up the actual texture of leadership: the standing meeting, the conversation you have been deferring, the unplanned moment that arrives without warning, the late-afternoon demand that finds you when your reserves are lowest. These are the rooms where formation is tested not by dramatic pressure but by sustained, undramatic, ordinary pressure that never announces itself as a test.

You finish the coffee. You pick up your keys. Something in your chest is already organizing itself for what is ahead, not the content, the content will take care of itself, but the quality of presence you will need to bring to rooms that may or may not be ready to receive it. The preparation that matters is no longer the material.

You drive. The route is automatic. Your mind does not rehearse the day. Your body does. It is already sensing what is coming, not the specifics, the texture. The weight of being watched. The effort of remaining available when the rooms ask for more than you are certain you have. The discipline of not performing what you cannot yet produce.

You pull into the lot. You sit for a moment before opening the door. Not because you need to gather yourself. Because this moment is still yours. In a few minutes, it will belong to the rooms. To the people in them. To whatever the work asks.

You open the door.

·　·　·

The meeting room is already half full.

You notice this before you notice who is in it. Not the faces. The room's weight. Something in the air that is not tension exactly but not ease either. A held quality, like a breath drawn in and not yet released. You have been in this meeting every Wednesday for months. You know who sits where, who speaks first, who waits. The room is familiar. What is different is that you feel it now, the way a musician walking onto a stage feels the audience before the lights come up.

You sit. You greet people. The ordinary exchanges, the small talk that is not small but structural, the brief eye contact that establishes: I see you, we are here, we can begin. You do this without thinking about it because you have done it a thousand times. But underneath the doing, something is registering. The person at the far end of the table who smiled when you walked in but whose shoulders did not move. The slight delay before someone responded to a question that should have been easy. The quality of the laughter, a half-beat too fast, as if the room is performing relaxation rather than experiencing it.

A year ago, this would have been background noise. Sensory data that arrived without a category and dissolved before it could be useful. Now it is foreground. Not because you are trying to read the room. Because the room is arriving in your body whether you want it to or not. Your chest has tightened slightly. Your breathing has shifted. Something in your posture has adjusted to accommodate what the room is holding. You did not decide to do any of this. The body decided. The body has been deciding for years, and you are only now aware of how much it carries on your behalf.

The meeting begins. The agenda is the same as last week. Updates, timelines, decisions that need to be made or deferred. Someone presents numbers. Someone asks a clarifying question. The rhythm is familiar, efficient, routine. The meeting is working.

And it is dead.

You can feel it. The room is performing productivity. Every item is addressed. Every question is answered. The pace is appropriate, the tone is professional, and the content is accurate. Nothing is wrong. And nothing is alive. The part of the room that takes risks, that says the unexpected thing, that pushes back because pushback is where the real thinking happens, that part left before the meeting started. What remains is agreement.

You sense this in your body before you can articulate it. A flatness in your sternum. A quality of attention that is like watching through glass, everything is visible, and nothing can be touched. The people in the room are present in body and absent in the way that matters. You have felt this before. You have a word for it now, a word the book gave you, but the word is less useful than the feeling. The feeling is precise. The word is approximate.

And here is the choice that did not use to exist.

A year ago the meeting would have proceeded and you would have let it proceed and you would not have known that anything was missing. The agenda would have been completed. The action items would have been assigned. Everyone would have left with the sense that the meeting was productive because productivity is what the room measured and by that measure it was fine.

Now you can feel what is missing. You can feel the gap between what the room is producing and what the room could hold if someone opened the door. If someone said the thing that is not on the agenda. If someone named the flatness, not as accusation but as observation. If someone asked the question that everyone in the room is carrying and no one has been willing to surface.

You know the question. You can feel its shape. It has something to do with the initiative that has stalled, the one no one wants to declare dead because declaring it dead means acknowledging that three months of work led nowhere. The room has been circling this for weeks, referencing it in euphemism, updating its timeline without updating its prognosis. The initiative is gone.

No one has said it. And the not-saying has become the room's actual climate, the held breath that you felt when you walked in.

You could say it. You have the standing. You have the words. You can feel them forming, simple, direct, honest: I think we need to acknowledge that this is not going to work. The sentence is right there. Your chest wants to open. Your voice wants to offer.

And you don't.

Not because you lack courage. Not because the moment passes too quickly. Because you can feel, in your body, not your mind, that the room is not ready. That the sentence, however true, would land as interruption rather than invitation. That the people in this room need to arrive at this truth through their own reckoning, not receive it from you. That offering it now, however, honestly, would be an act of your need to be the person who names things, not an act of service to what the room actually requires.

This distinction would have been invisible to you before. The impulse to speak and the discernment about whether speaking serves, these used to be the same thing. If you felt it, you said it. If the truth was clear, you offered it. Now you can feel the impulse and hold it separately from the action. The gap between sensing and responding has widened by half a second. And in that half-second, something that is not quite wisdom but is closer to judgment tells you: not yet. Not this room. Not today.

You let the meeting proceed.

The agenda concludes. The action items are confirmed. People gather their things. Someone makes a joke on the way out. The room empties.

You sit for a moment. The meeting was fine. The meeting was dead. You could feel both of these things simultaneously, and you could not change either of them. The formation gave you sight. It did not give you permission to act on what you saw. And the weight of seeing clearly inside a room that is not ready to see itself is its own kind of carrying.

You stand. You walk toward the next room. The weight comes with you.

•   •   •

The conversation is at eleven. You have known about it for a week. You have been preparing for it without preparing for it, which is to say it has been running in the background of your body the way a low-frequency sound runs beneath everything else in a room. Not loud enough to demand attention. Present enough to alter the texture of every other thing you do.

This is someone you chose. You advocated for them. You saw something in them that others were not yet sure about, and you made the case, and the case was persuasive, and now, four months later, the thing you saw is not what is showing up. The numbers are part of it but not the center of it. The center of it is something you can feel when they present in meetings, a thinness, a slight over-preparation that signals effort where there should be ground. They are working harder than they should need to. You recognize this because you have done it yourself. The compensating. The effortful steadiness that substitutes for the steadiness that was supposed to be there by now.

You have not named this to them. You have been waiting, telling yourself you are giving them time, telling yourself the role needs a full two quarters to settle, telling yourself that raising it too early would undermine the confidence they are still building. Some of this is true. Some of it is the story you are telling yourself because the alternative, sitting across from someone you believe in and naming what you both can feel, requires a quality of presence you are not certain you have for this particular conversation. It is easier to hold a room of strangers than to hold a room with one person who trusts you.

Eleven o'clock. They sit down. Their posture is composed, prepared, a slight forward lean that communicates engagement. You notice it because you notice everything now. The lean is a fraction too deliberate. The eye contact is steady in the way that managed eye contact is steady. They have prepared for this meeting too, you realize. They have been carrying their own version of the background frequency. They know something is coming. They may not know what. But their body knows.

You begin with the ordinary. The check-in. The open question. How are things going. You ask this not as preamble but as a genuine inquiry, and you listen not to the words but to what is underneath the words. Their answer is competent. Organized. They lead with what is working. They name a challenge but frame it as progress. The narrative is coherent. The body is not.

You can feel the discrepancy. Their words are moving forward, and something in them is bracing. A tension in the jaw. A quality of stillness in the hands that is not calm but held. You have seen this before, in others, in yourself. The body's preparation for the moment when the conversation turns. The held breath before the thing that has not yet been said.

This is where attunement becomes precise and dangerous. You can sense what they are carrying. You can feel the fear beneath the competence, the question they cannot ask: Am I failing? Is this the conversation where you tell me? The question is not in their words. It is in the half-second pause before each answer, in the care with which each sentence is constructed, in the way their eyes hold yours a beat too long, looking for something, reassurance or truth, and not sure which they want.

A year ago, you would have sensed something vague. Discomfort. Nervousness. General unease. You would have responded to the general shape of it, offered reassurance or redirection, and the conversation would have stayed on the surface where both of you could manage it.

Now the sensing is specific. You can feel the precise contour of what they are holding. And specificity creates obligation. When you can feel exactly what someone carries, you become responsible to it in a way that vague sensing never demands. The vague sense allows you to address the category. The specific sense asks you to address the person.

You listen longer than you used to. You let the silence after their answer extend by a beat, not as technique, not because you read somewhere that silence creates space, but because your body tells you the next words matter and they have not yet arrived. You are waiting for something. Not the right thing to say. The right place to say it from. The difference is everything. The words you could offer from your mind are accurate, constructive, professionally appropriate. The words you are waiting for come from somewhere else, from the place where your perception of their struggle meets your own experience of having struggled, where the observation and the care are not separate things but a single coherent response.

The words arrive. You begin to speak.

And they come out slightly wrong.

Not the content. The content is close. But the tone carries a fraction too much care, or a fraction too little directness, you cannot tell which. Something in your voice signals that you are managing this moment rather than standing inside it. You hear it as you speak. A smoothness that is not dishonest but is not fully present either. The sentence that was supposed to open a door opens it at a slight angle, and the angle matters, because the person across from you is listening not to your words but to whether you are actually in the room with them or performing being in the room with them.

You can feel their response before it becomes visible. A micro-settling. The forward lean that was a fraction too deliberate becomes a fraction more guarded. They are still listening. They have not closed. But the opening you sensed, the opening where the real conversation might have happened, has narrowed. Not shut. Narrowed. By the width of whatever it was in your voice that signaled management rather than presence.

The conversation continues. It is honest, mostly. You say things that are true and they hear them. You name what you have observed and they receive it with composure. There are moments where the room softens, where something almost surfaces, where you can feel the possibility of the conversation becoming the conversation it wants to be. And each time, the possibility recedes, not because either of you retreats, but because the opening requires a precision of presence that you can almost sustain but not quite. Not today. Not with this person who trusts you. Not with the weight of your own investment in their success sitting in your chest alongside the weight of what you need to say.

The conversation ends. It was productive. It was professional. It moved things forward.

It was not the conversation it could have been.

You both know this. It goes unnamed. They will leave and sit with what you said and some of it will land and some of it will be filtered through the slight guardedness that your tone created. You will sit with the knowledge that the attunement worked, you felt what was there, you sensed the precise shape of what they carried, and the capacity to translate that sensing into what the moment required was not yet fully formed.

Two things are true. You were closer than you have ever been to the conversation this person needed. And closer is not there.

You stand. Something in your shoulders has tightened. Not from conflict. From the specific weight of having almost held what the room asked you to hold. The almost is heavier than failure. Failure is clean. Almost lingers. You can feel exactly where your capacity ended and performance began, and the seam between them is visible now, visible to you, and you cannot be sure it was not visible to them.

You walk toward the next room. The day is half over. The weight is not.

· · ·

You are between rooms. The eleven o'clock is behind you. The afternoon is ahead. There is a window of thirty minutes that belongs to no one, and you are using it the way you use most unscheduled time: sitting at your desk, not quite working, not quite resting. Your body is metabolizing the conversation, replaying not the words but the sensations, the moment your tone shifted, the narrowing you felt, the weight of almost. You are not analyzing. You are absorbing.

Someone appears at your door.

Not on the calendar. Not expected. The knock is soft, almost apologetic, and you know before you look up that this is not administrative. Something in the quality of the knock tells you that the person standing there needs something that is not on any agenda.

You look up. One of your team leads. They are standing in the doorway the way people stand when they are not sure they have the right to be there. One hand on the frame. Weight on the back foot.

You don't give them a reason to leave.

You gesture. They sit. And for a moment, neither of you speaks. The silence is brief, three seconds, maybe four, but it is not empty. Something is being decided in the space between you. Not by you. By them. Whether this is safe. Whether what they are carrying can be set down here.

Your body makes a choice. You do not lean forward. You do not tilt your head in the practiced gesture of active listening. You settle. Your weight drops slightly in the chair. Your hands, which were on the keyboard, come to rest in your lap. Your breath, which had been shallow from the morning's accumulation, drops into your belly. None of this is conscious. None of it is technique. It is what your body does now, after years of being in rooms where someone needed something they could not name.

They begin to talk. Not about work. About work. The words are about a project, a timeline, a colleague. But the words are not the thing. The thing is underneath the words, in the slight tremor at the edge of the voice, in the way the sentences circle without landing, in the effort to frame as professional something that is personal. Something has shifted for this person in a way that is affecting everything, and they are trying to bring it to you in the only language the workplace allows.

You listen. Not for the problem. For the person. This is a distinction you could not have made five years ago. Five years ago you would have heard the project concern and addressed the project concern and the person would have left with a solution to the thing they did not actually come to talk about. You would have been helpful. You would have missed them.

They pause. The pause is longer than the ones between sentences. It is the pause where the decision happens. You can feel it in your own chest, a slight tightening, the body's recognition that the next moment matters. They are at the edge of something. You have been at this edge yourself. You know that what happens next depends not on what you say but on what you are.

You hold the silence. Not as strategy. As presence. Your breath is steady. Your attention is on them without being pointed at them, a quality of attention that holds without gripping, that is available without being intrusive.

They speak. What comes out is not the whole truth. It is a piece of it. A sentence, maybe two, that moves past the project language and touches something real. Something about feeling overwhelmed in a way they cannot explain. Something about doubting whether they are in the right role. Something that, a year ago, they would never have said in this room, to this person, during a workday.

They said it because the room held.

You respond. You do not fix. You do not reassure. You do not offer the sentence that would make this easier for both of you. Instead, you say something simple. Something that acknowledges what they said without interpreting it, without rushing past it, without making it smaller than it is.

You are not sure the words are right. You are never sure. But they came from a place that was not performing. For a moment, a brief one, you were not managing the encounter. You were inside it.

They nod. Something in their shoulders releases. Not dramatically. A fraction. An exhale that is slightly longer than the one before it. They are not fixed. The thing they are carrying has not been resolved. But it has been witnessed. And witnessed, it weighs differently than it weighed when they were carrying it alone.

They stand. A nod, a word. They leave. The room is quiet.

You sit in the quiet. Something happened. Not something you can report, not something that will appear in any metric, not something anyone will ever know about. A person came to your door carrying something they could not name, and you held the room, and they set a piece of it down, and the setting down was possible because of who you were in that room, not what you said or did.

It was enough for this room.

The afternoon is still ahead.

•   •   •

It arrives at three-fifteen.

Not as crisis. As accumulation. The call that was supposed to be routine turns. The voice on the other end is someone senior to you, and the information they are delivering reorganizes the next six months. Not catastrophically. Not in the way that produces emergency meetings and urgent all-hands communications. In the way that produces a slow, heavy understanding that what you have been building is no longer what is being asked for. The strategic direction has shifted. The shift is reasonable. The reasoning is sound. And the weight of it, the weight of knowing what this means for the people who have been working inside the old direction, who trusted it because you told them to trust it, who invested in it because you asked them to invest, that weight arrives in your body all at once, in the chest, in the space behind the eyes, in the sudden heaviness of your arms on the desk.

The call ends. You have thirty minutes before a meeting where several of those people will be in the room. They do not yet know. You are now the person who knows and has not yet told them. You are holding it alone for now. The timing is not right. The meeting is not the place. But the meeting will happen, and you will be in the room with people who do not know what you know, and your body will be holding what they cannot yet see.

You walk into the meeting. Your body is performing steadiness. You can feel it performing. This is different from the earlier rooms. In the morning meeting, the formation allowed you to see what the room held. In the conversation at eleven, the formation brought you close to the intervention the moment needed. In the unplanned visit, the formation was there, available, sufficient.

Here, the formation is not sufficient.

You can feel the difference. It is not dramatic. It is the difference between standing on ground and standing on something that gives slightly under each step. Your voice is steady but you can hear the thinness in it, a quality of control that is not calm but managed calm. Your body is present in the room but a part of your attention is devoted to the carrying, to the knowledge that sits behind your sternum like a held breath, and that attention is not available for the people in front of you. You are divided. Not visibly. But structurally. The part of you that holds what they do not know and the part of you that must be present to them are drawing from the same reservoir, and the reservoir, after this day, after this week, after the morning's weight and the almost of the eleven o'clock and the unplanned visit that asked for everything your settling could offer, the reservoir is not full.

Someone asks you a question. It is a good question. It deserves a real answer, an answer that comes from the place where your understanding of the work and your presence in the room meet. You reach for that place.

It is not there.

What is there is competence. Skill. The practiced ability to construct an answer that is accurate, responsive, appropriate. You hear yourself deliver it. The answer is fine. The room receives it. No one looks twice.

But you felt the reaching. You felt the moment when your hand closed on air. The capacity to answer from presence, from the place where what you know and who you are in this room are integrated, was not available. What was available was the performance layer. The layer that has always been there, reliable, professional, adequate. The layer you can feel now with painful precision because the formation has given you the sensitivity to know when you are operating from it and when you are operating from something deeper.

You are operating from the layer. Not from the ground.

The meeting continues. You participate. You track the conversation. You offer input where input is needed. And underneath the participation, you are aware of the gap, the distance between what you are producing and what these people deserve, which is not your management of this moment but your presence inside it.

There is a moment, midway through, when someone says something honest. An observation about the work that is more vulnerable than the room usually allows. It is the kind of moment the earlier part of this day prepared you for, the kind of moment where your settling, your attention, your willingness to hold what surfaces could change what happens next. The room pauses. The opening is there.

And you cannot meet it.

Your body tries. You feel the impulse to settle, to offer the quality of presence that held the room an hour ago when someone appeared at your door. But the settling does not come. The breath stays shallow. The weight behind your sternum does not release. You are too full. The day has asked too much and the carrying has consumed the capacity that this moment needs. You respond, and the response is appropriate, and the moment passes, and the opening closes, and the person who said the honest thing receives not your presence but your professionalism, which is a different thing, and their body knows it is a different thing, and something in the room adjusts.

The meeting ends. People leave. You remain.

You are sitting in an empty room, and the day is pressing against you from the inside. Not the events of the day. The weight of having been the person who moved through those events. The morning's dead meeting that you saw clearly and could not change. The conversation that almost opened and did not. The unplanned visit where the formation held. And now this: the room where it did not.

The capacity was there this morning. It was there at eleven, imperfectly. It was there when someone knocked on your door. But capacity draws from a reservoir that the day depletes. The breath stays shallow. The settling does not come. You wait for it anyway. It does not arrive.

You continue.

•　　•　　•

You sit in the car.

The engine is running. You have not put it in gear. The parking lot is emptying around you, and you are sitting with your hands on the wheel, and your body is doing something it does at the end of these days, a slow unwinding that is not relaxation but release, the way a muscle that has been clenched for hours does not relax so much as surrender. Your shoulders drop. Your jaw, which has been set since the three-fifteen meeting, loosens. Your breath finds its way back to your belly.

You are not processing the day. The day is processing you. It moves through your body in no particular order: the flatness of the morning meeting, the almost of the eleven o'clock, the moment someone knocked on your door, and you were there for them, the moment in the afternoon when you were not. These are not thoughts. They are sensations. The morning's flatness sits in your chest as a kind of dull weight. The almost sits on your shoulders. The moment of presence sits somewhere warmer, quieter, harder to locate. The afternoon's insufficiency sits everywhere.

You are tired. Not the tired that sleep fixes. The tired that lives in the space between who you were today and who the day needed you to be. The gap was small in some rooms. In one room, it was nearly closed. In one room, it was too wide. The gap is always there. The formation has not eliminated it. The formation has made you capable of feeling it with precision, and precision is not comfort. Precision is the specific weight of knowing exactly where your capacity ended, and your performance began, and carrying that knowledge home in a body that held what it could and could not hold what it couldn't and did not break.

You did not break. This matters, though it does not feel like it matters. It feels ordinary. It feels like the minimum. But the minimum, after a day like this, after the accumulated weight of rooms that asked for everything and received what was available, the minimum is not nothing. The minimum is what formation built. Not the capacity to hold everything. The capacity to remain intact when you cannot.

The lot is almost empty. The light has changed. You notice the light because your body is beginning to return to you now, returning from the rooms, from the people, from the carrying. For a moment, you are aware of yourself in a way that the day did not permit. Not as a leader. Not as the person who holds. As a body in a car in a parking lot at the end of a Wednesday, tired in a way that has no language, carrying what the day left behind.

You put the car in gear. You drive home.

The day is in your body. The work continues.

NINE
What I Saw

The witness's testimony

I didn't set out to study artists.

I wasn't looking for a theory, or a framework, or a missing variable in leadership research. I was trying to understand a feeling I had carried for years, one that showed up most clearly in moments when leadership mattered most and felt least reliable.

It appeared in rooms where everyone was competent and nothing moved. In leaders who were admired, prepared, ethical, and somehow unable to hold the moment when it arrived.

I saw it first as absence, not insight.

Something would thin. Attention would scatter. People would retreat into performance, saying the right things, nodding, complying, while the real work slipped out of reach.

I came to think of it as a kind of polite leaving. Everyone was still in the room. But the part of them that could be reached, the part that takes risks, tells difficult truths, invests something personal in the outcome, had already gone.

At the time, I assumed this was a failure of execution, or courage, or clarity. That's what leadership language offered me. If something wasn't working, the answer was more alignment, better communication, sharper incentives, clearer vision.

So I learned those things. I taught them. I watched others do the same.

And still, the same failures repeated, not loudly, not dramatically, but quietly and consistently. The kind of failure that doesn't look like collapse, but like erosion. People stayed. The work continued. But something essential withdrew.

•　　•　　•

I didn't yet have language for what I was noticing. I only knew that the leaders who held these moments, who could stay present without tightening, who could speak without inflaming, who could let uncertainty exist without rushing to fill it, were doing something different.

They weren't smarter. They weren't more charismatic. They weren't better prepared.

They were different in themselves.

•   •   •

I saw it first in places that weren't called leadership at all.

In a small rehearsal room, watching a dancer reset after a mistake, not with apology or self-protection, but with a kind of grounded attentiveness that brought the entire room back with her. The space was warm. The floor was scuffed. She had missed a transition badly enough that the pianist stopped. And for a moment, the air held that particular silence, the one where everyone waits to see whether the person exposed will shrink or recover. She did neither. She stood still. She breathed. And then she began again from a place that was quieter than where she'd been before the mistake, and somehow the whole room lowered with her. I remember thinking: I have watched executives try to do exactly that after a failed quarter, and none of them knew how.

In a workshop where a potter lifted a cracked vessel from the wheel and held it for the group to see. The crack ran from the rim nearly to the base. She said nothing. She turned the vessel slowly, studying the flaw the way you might study a face. Then she pressed her thumb along the crack, not to close it but to widen it slightly, and the vessel became something else. The flaw was no longer a failure. It was a feature of the form. She had changed her relationship to what was broken, and we could feel it.

In a jazz trio where the structure dissolved mid-performance. The bassist had moved to a different key. The pianist followed, but the drummer hadn't heard the shift. For four or five bars, three musicians were playing in three different places. I watched the audience tense, the collective inhale of people sensing something going wrong. And then, instead of stopping or forcing alignment, the three musicians did something I had never seen a leadership team do: they listened harder. Not to correct each other. To find each other. The drummer softened. The pianist simplified. The bassist repeated a phrase, once, twice, until it became an anchor. Within thirty seconds, a new coherence emerged that was better than what they'd planned. No one led the recovery in the usual way. The recovery was the listening itself.

No one called these moments leadership. But people leaned in. They trusted. They followed.

·   ·   ·

I began to notice that artists spent an enormous amount of time training for moments like this, moments where there is no script, where visibility is unavoidable, where failure is public, where the body reacts before the mind can intervene.

They didn't train to avoid pressure. They trained inside it.

What struck me was not their talent, but their relationship to exposure. Artists expected to be seen before they were ready. To fail without explanation. To stay in contact with the work even when it resisted them.

They became steadier, not rigid, not detached, but available. They developed a sensitivity to timing that couldn't be taught in words. They learned when to push and when to pause, when to hold silence, and when to intervene.

Most importantly, they learned how to remain themselves when the moment asked something unexpected of them.

·   ·   ·

The same quality appeared in leaders who could hold difficult moments without collapsing or controlling them. Leaders who could sit in tension without rushing to relieve it. Who could name uncertainty without amplifying fear. Who could allow disagreement without needing to win.

I remember one in particular. A manufacturing executive, the morning after announcing a plant closure that would eliminate a hundred and forty jobs. He had to walk the floor. Not to explain, the explanation had been given the day before. Not to reassure, there was nothing reassuring to say. He had to be present to people who were angry and afraid and who had every reason to look at him as the source of their pain. I watched him stop at a machine where a woman had worked for nineteen years. She didn't look up. He didn't speak. He stood there, not performing compassion, not projecting strength, just standing in the full weight of what he had done and what it cost. After a long moment, she looked at him. He met her eyes. Something passed between them that I cannot name but that I recognized instantly: it was the same thing I had seen in the dancer after the stumble. A willingness to be present to what was real without reaching for what was comfortable.

When I asked him later how he learned to do that, he didn't talk about models or programs. Neither did any of the others, the handful of leaders I encountered over the years who carried this same quality.

They talked about experience. About being stretched. About moments that cost them something.

About learning, often painfully, what happened in their bodies under pressure, and how to stay.

•　　•　　•

What I saw, slowly and unmistakably, was that leadership had inherited no serious developmental pathway for this kind of formation.

We trained people to decide, to plan, to communicate, to analyze. We rarely trained them to be visible without armor. To sense what was happening beneath the words. To hold meaning when facts were insufficient.

Artists, on the other hand, lived inside those demands. Not as metaphor but as daily practice.

They rehearsed not just technique, but recovery. Not just expression, but restraint. Not just creativity, but responsibility to an audience, a space, a moment.

•　　•　　•

What I was seeing was not artistry as expression, but artistry as formation.

A slow reshaping of attention. Not the attention that focuses on a task, but the wider attention that holds a room, that senses the shift before it surfaces, that feels the temperature of a conversation the way a musician feels the tempo of a piece. Artists trained this attention not by thinking about it but by practicing inside conditions that demanded it. Night after night. Rehearsal after rehearsal. Until the attention was no longer effortful but structural, part of who they were, not something they turned on.

A recalibration of the nervous system. The body learns before the mind. Artists who had performed under exposure for years had nervous systems that responded to pressure differently, not with the freeze or flight that untrained bodies default to, but with a settling, an opening, a readiness that allowed them to act from presence rather than react from fear. This was not courage in the way we usually mean it. It was physiology. It was what the body becomes when it has practiced being seen enough times to stop treating visibility as a threat.

A training in presence that held even when everything else wavered.

Later, when I sat with artists across sixteen disciplines and asked not what they made but what making had made of them, the findings confirmed what I had been watching for decades. The same capacities. The same formation arc. The same interior architecture, built through sustained practice, that the leaders who held difficult moments had somehow acquired, and the leaders who struggled had not.

The research gave the seeing language. But the seeing came first.

•   •   •

And I saw, clearly now, that leadership had been asking for this without knowing where to find it.

The leaders who struggled weren't failing because they lacked insight. They were failing because the situations they faced required capacities that had never been built.

The leaders who held weren't exceptional because they knew more. They were different because they had practiced becoming someone who could stay.

What I saw, again and again, was this:

When the room grew tense, some people tightened and transmitted that tension outward. Others absorbed it and changed the field.

When identity was threatened, some people defended the role. Others stood somewhere deeper and allowed something new to emerge.

When meaning fractured, some people filled the space with explanation. Others offered something quieter, an image, a story, a pause, that helped people reorient.

No competency model could explain the difference.

But practice could.

•   •   •

The artists knew this. They had always known it.

They did not ask, "What should I do when this happens?"

They asked, "Who must I become to meet this moment?"

Leadership had been asking the first question for a century.

This book begins with the second.

EPILOGUE
The Willingness to Return

This book was written over many years, but it began in a single moment.

I was standing in the back of a theater, not a grand one, a community space with folding chairs and a stage that creaked, watching a dress rehearsal fall apart. The lead actress forgot her lines. The lighting cue came late. A prop broke. And the director, a woman I had known for years, did not stop the rehearsal. She sat in the third row and watched. She did not correct. She did not intervene. She held.

And the cast found their way back. Not immediately. Not elegantly. But they found it, through listening, through adjusting, through the accumulated practice of having been in rooms where things broke and where the only option was to stay and work it through.

Afterward, I asked her why she hadn't stopped them. She said something I have never forgotten: "Because they needed to learn that they could survive it. And they can't learn that if I rescue them."

That sentence is the spine of this book.

•　　•　　•

I owe debts I cannot repay.

To the artists across sixteen disciplines who sat with the research and answered questions about the most private dimension of their work, not what they made, but what making had made of them. Their honesty was extraordinary. Their willingness to describe the interior of formation, the cost of it, the loneliness of it, the way it changes what you see without giving you the language to explain what you now see, gave this body of work its ground.

To the leaders who shared their failures. Not their successes, their failures. The rooms they could not hold. The silences they misjudged. The meaning they offered too early. The presence that arrived too late. It is easier to speak about what worked. The leaders who spoke about what did not work, who allowed the research to enter the places where their capacity was insufficient, made this book honest in a way it could not otherwise have been.

To the people in the rooms described in these pages who did not know they were being watched and who taught me what no curriculum could. The dancer who breathed. The potter who widened the crack. The jazz musicians who listened harder. The manufacturing executive who stood at the machine and did not speak. I have carried these moments for years. They are the evidence I trust most.

•   •   •

I am still learning.

I do not write this from a place of mastery. I write it from the same place the book asks the reader to stand, inside the ongoing condition of a work that demands more than I have been formed to offer, and that I return to anyway.

Last month, I was in a room where the holding was required, and my capacity was not sufficient. The room needed something from me that I could feel but could not produce. I reached for meaning too early. I felt the room close. I drove home carrying the weight of it.

I tell you this not as confession but as credential. The only credential that matters in a book about formation is ongoing contact with the work. Not having arrived. Not having mastered. Having returned.

The willingness to return is not the end of the story. It is the only chapter that never finishes.

•   •   •

In time, I will name the framework more fully and present the research that gave the seeing its language. The evidence matters. The developmental architecture matters. But I wanted this book to come first. Because the seeing came first. Before the framework, before the evidence, before the theory, there was a person standing in a room, watching another person hold what could not be held through logic or planning or force, and thinking: I need to understand what I just saw.

If you have read this far, you have seen it too. In the rooms you have led. In the moments you have held, or failed to hold. In the weight you carry home and cannot name.

The work continues.

It asks what it has always asked.

Who must I become to meet this moment?

Author's Note on Sources

This book does not cite its sources in the conventional sense. That is a deliberate choice, not an oversight. The argument is grounded in research, but the text is written to be experienced rather than annotated. What follows is an honest accounting of the intellectual traditions and bodies of evidence that informed the work.

The understanding of formation that runs through these pages draws from phenomenological research traditions, particularly the study of lived experience as a valid and rigorous form of inquiry into how human beings are changed by sustained practice. The qualitative research at the heart of this work involved extended interviews with artists across sixteen disciplines, asking not what they made but what making had made of them. That research confirmed patterns I had observed for decades and gave the observation its structure.

The neuroscience referenced throughout the book, particularly regarding the nervous system's response to pressure, exposure, and uncertainty, draws from research in stress physiology, embodied cognition, and the growing literature on interoception and somatic awareness. I have relied especially on work that examines how the body processes threat and safety beneath conscious awareness, and how repeated exposure under practice conditions can recalibrate that processing over time.

The leadership scholarship that this book both builds on and departs from includes developmental leadership theory, adaptive leadership, complexity leadership, and the substantial literature on leader identity and identity threat. The argument is not that this scholarship is wrong. It is that it has been incomplete in ways that become visible only when you look at what artistic formation traditions have been quietly building for centuries.

The artistic formation traditions themselves, apprenticeship models, studio pedagogy, rehearsal-based learning, critique as developmental practice, carry deep knowledge that has rarely been translated into leadership language. This book attempts that translation without reducing what it translates. The traditions deserve more than I can offer here. The volumes that follow will engage them more fully.

I have not listed specific titles or authors because the register of this book does not accommodate that kind of apparatus. Readers who wish to pursue the research underlying these ideas will find a more complete engagement with the evidence in subsequent volumes of this emerging canon, published under the Threshold Leadership imprint.

ABOUT THE AUTHOR

David S. Morgan has spent three decades watching what happens to human beings under the pressure of work that will not relent. He has led organizations across manufacturing, technology, and the nonprofit sector, standing in rooms where institutional survival was decided and where the capacity to hold what the moment required was either present or it was not.

He began noticing what artists carried that leaders had never been trained to build. That noticing became a research program, a body of writing, and an ongoing practice of returning to the demand.

He writes about formation: what sustained contact with difficult work does to the person who stays inside it. He writes not from mastery but from the same condition the book describes, the ongoing work of becoming sufficient for what the work requires.

He lives in New Hampshire. He is still learning.

Other books by the author include *AI-Proof Manifesto*, *The Joy of Discontent*, *Designing in the Dark*, *Tending to Our Fire*, *Flip the TWITCH*, and *Shaker*.